Harlem Godfather: The Rap on my Husband, Ellsworth "Bumpy" Johnson

by Mayme Hatcher Johnson
and Karen E. Quinones Miller

Oshun Publishing Company, Inc.
Philadelphia

Mayme Johnson
and Karen E. Quinones Miller

Also by Karen E. Quinones Miller

Satin Doll
I'm Telling
Using What You Got
Ida B.
Uptown Dreams
Satin Nights
Passin'

Harlem Godfather:
The Rap on my Husband, Ellsworth "Bumpy" Johnson

Oshun Publishing Company, Inc.
7715 Crittenden Street
Box 377
Philadelphia, PA 19118

First Edition: March 2008

10 9 8 7 6 5 4 3 2 1

visit the Harlem Godfather website at www.harlemgodfather.com

cover design by Linda Ballard

Mayme Johnson
and Karen E. Quinones Miller

This book is lovingly dedicated to:

My husband . . .
Bumpy, when God made you he broke the mold.
I will always love you, and you are forever in
my heart and on my mind.

and to my great grandson, Anthony Hatcher
Johnson. . .
Continue to follow your dreams, so; it's the
only way to reach the stars!

Harlem Godfather:

The Rap on my Husband, Ellsworth "Bumpy" Johnson

Mayme Hatcher Johnson
and
Karen E. Quinones Miller

Oshun Publishing Company, Inc.
Philadelphia

<u>Acknowledgements – Mayme Hatcher Johnson</u>

I'd like to start off by thanking Mr. Henry "Perk" Perkins who cared about this book as much as if it was his own. Perk, you've always been a good friend, and I truly appreciate you.

I also want to thank Margaret and Anthony Johnson, my granddaughter and great-grandson, for their support and help during the writing of this book.

And I can't forget all of my nieces and nephews, but especially Love Crawley, Shana Parker, Cecelia Steppe Jones, and Ron Burroughs. I also have to mention Tony Paige, who's been like a nephew to me, and his daughter and my goddaughter, Eileen Paige.

Of course I have to acknowledge my good friends Doris Bowlin, Belinda Taylor and Flo Polk. You all have been loyal friends throughout the years, and I feel blessed to know all three of you. And I can't forget Veradelle Chance, my oldest friend – thanks for being in my life.

This would also be a good time to also thank J. J. Johnson and Lovey Hamilton, whom I've also known for more than 50 years. And I can't forget Brian Pope who has also been a loyal friend.

"Spanish" Raymond Marquez, it was good talking to you again after all these years. Let's stay in touch.

But in addition to my old friends, I'd also like to take this time to acknowledge my new young friends – Tameka Garner, Gail Davis, Theresa Brunson, Anthony "Tone" Gonzalez, and Camille Miller (with her cute self!). Being around all of you keeps me young.

And last but not least I want to thank Karen E. Quinones Miller, my co-author and my friend. Karen we've been talking about doing this book for almost twenty years now. Finally it's done. God Bless You.

Acknowledgements – Karen E. Quinones Miller

As usual I have to thank the members of the Evening Star Writer's Group. Shalena Broaster, Theresa Brunson, Bahiya Cabral-Johnson, Fiona Harewood -- I don't know what I would have done without your advice and critiques as the book was shaping up. It's no wonder that Evening Star is considered Philadelphia's premiere writing group.

Much thanks, also, to my cousin Adrian Thomas, who was kind enough to go over the manuscript time and time again. And I also thank Sherlane Freeman, who went over it yet again.

I give special thanks, as does Mrs. Johnson, to Henry "Perk" Perkins – the legendary Harlem club owner and restaurateur – who went well above and beyond to make sure this book happened. Perk, I can't wait to read YOUR book!

And I thank Linda Ballard who designed the wonderful Harlem Godfather book cover free of charge, and Makeda Smith of Jazzmyne Public Relations – who didn't know us but reached out with an offer of help because she thought this a project that needed to be supported.

To bestselling author Shannon Holmes: You are a wonderful, wonderful person, and I'm so glad I know you. Of all the people in the literary world who said they would do whatever they could to make this project happen, Shannon was the only one who actually came through. Thank you, dear friend!

I give special thanks to all those who pre-paid for copies of this book in order for us to have the money to get it done. You have my deepest appreciation.

But most of all I thank Mrs. Mayme Johnson – just knowing you has truly enriched my life.

Thanking Those Who Made This Book Happen!

Adam Amaro; Adonis Cooper; Agnes M. Lee; Albert
Gunn; Alexander Rios ; Alexis Dobbins; Alfred Oglesby;
Alvin Alexis; Andrew Roane; Angela Jefferson; Anthony
Krigbaum; Anthony Morris; Anya Lindsey; Aristotle
Stathatos; Armahn Britt; Arno Icon Troxler; Arturo
Varela Jr.; Asiatic Allah; Asukaya Bailey; Athena Rosa
McMillan; Audrey Morrissette; Barbara Milhouse; Becky
Dial; Bernard Potter; Betty J. Shabazz; Bobbie Chestand;
Booker T. Johnson, Jr.; Brett Bradford; Burnside 183rd Fat
Cat; Butter; Carlton Davis: Carol Ann Haynes; Celess
Martin; Celosia Singleton; Charlene Butler Perry; Charles
Kogan; Charlie "E-Z" Davis; Chaterral Stovall; Christian
Aliperti; Clarence E. Jones Jr./AKA "CLAY"; Clarence
Malik Mohammed; Clarence Sylvester; Clyde Lewis;
Collier Harris; Coney Braddy ; Consuerella Chaney;
Cornel M Williams; Craig Smith; Cynthia Moore; D. T.
Bullock; Darin Lee Sympton; Darnetta Frazier ; David
Partridge; David Shellman NYC; David Williams; Davon
Stephenson; Dear Sisters Literary Group; Deborah Evans;
Deborah Lee ; Debra Dishmon; Delf's Al Day
Promotions; Dell Jones; Delores Jenkins; Denise McFall;
Derrick Randolph; Dianne Washington; DJ McTom;
Dwight A. Love; Earl Jordan; Edelmiro Perez; Edward T
Coley; Elizaida Galarza; Elvirita Lopez; Emma Claire
Gomersall; Emma Marbley; Eric Cherryhill; Eric Dee
Pittman; Eric M Hare; Eric Thomas; Erica Wright; Ester
B Williams; Fabricio "FAB-BROOKLYN" Marin;
Felecia Gunn; Florence M. Adams; Foster Zeh; Frances
Mahee; Frank J Valentine; Frank Oglesby; Franklin D.

Brown; Fylicia Rolland; G. Banks Entertainment;
gameofficial.com; Gary Jones; Gayle Sloan; Geoffrey
Ellis; George Michael; Gerald Henderson; Gracie
McKeever; Gregory Everett; Gregory Waters; Gregory
Zigler – Harlem World 146[th;] Gregoryjo Beasley; Gryphon
Dickerson; Harry Grent; Hassan Idris Muhammad;
Hassan Jackson; Hector Santiago; Helena Larry; Henrietta
J. Tate; Henry Barrington; Hinton Stephens; Homer
Keaton ; Howard J Jefferson; Howard Johnson; Hursell
Dolly; Irving Wright; Isaac Williams; Ishmael Rahman;
Jack Buckles; Jacqueline Beasley; Jacqueline Johnson;
Jacqueline Mathews; Jacqueline Waiters; Jalal Johnson;
Jamal Lee; Jamal Smalls aka Makavile "DA" Don; James
Bacon; James E Harris; James Sanchez; Jaromir Krol;
Jason Williams; Jeff Benson; Jefferey White; Jennelle
Evans; Jermario Hamilton; Jerry Butler; Jeweleen Perry;
Joann Bell; Jody Jones; Joe "The Man" Wells; John
Baillie; John D. Douglas; John E. Walden; John Fisher;
John Seay; Johnny Gibbs; Jose Samaniego; Joseph
Blandford; Joseph Byrd; Joseph Harrison; Joseph Marino;
Josh Silber; Joshua A. Maloy; Joyce Tate; Juanita McGill
"Juanita-Willie"; Judy Zeh; Julia Gooden; Justin Jordan;
Kamilah Collins; Keith N Johnson; Kellice Seymore;
Kenneth Williams; Kim Robinson; Kim Woods; Kurell
"NYMESIS" Brown; Kyel Windslow (Yahua, be Smart &
Brave!), Kyle Gray; Kyle Kennedy; Kyle Winslow;
Landton Malone; LaNell Bell; Larry McCall; LaShonda
Lee-Campbell; Lashunda Rogers; Leonard Smith; Leslie
Bethel; Loreia Johnson-Flemister; Linda Smith; Lou
DeQuesada; Luis Gyles; Luther Smith; Lydia Sutton;
Lynette Denson; M. Earl Johnson; Mack "Almalik"
Toliver; Macy Hake; Makeda Smith; Malcolm Freeney;
Mamie R Anderson; Marcella Banks; Maria Kusak; Mark
Bryant; Marq A. Harley; Marquine Lang; Mary Aliaga;
Mary Nichols; Matthew Angers; Michael "Baby Mike"
Patterson; Michael B. Harley; Michael Cartwright;
Michael Crawford; Michael Dixon; Michael F. Woods;

Michael J. Ryals; Michael Roe; Michael Waddell; Monte; MV's Wiggout Barbers; NaKeia Grimes; Nandi Crawford; Nathan Jones; Nathaniel Jones; Nelson Spellman; Nichole Jones; Nicole Staggers; Nicole Stevenson; O-Luv Money Productions; Oscar Huerta; Pamela L. Thomas; Parnell L. Johnson; Patricia Worthman; Patrick Coffey; Patrick D. Wilson; Paul Alston; Paul and Sara Bergman; Phew; Pitbull Palace; Qadir Muhammad; R J Grant; Ralph Cook; Rebecca Kendrick; Reginald B. Stewart; Rickie Jarrett; Rita Myers; Robert Barclay; Robert Delaney II; Roberto Berdeguer; Roman Valdespino; Ronald Bennafield; Ronell Mitchell, Sr.; Ronnie Burpo; Ronnie Coley; RootWomin/Iya O Karade; Rosanne Mack; Roy Jones; Rudy Grent; Ruth Estime; Samuel Dawson; Samuel Pledger; Sascha Schmitt; Scott Burke; Scott Haskins; Semril James; Shani White; Shannon Horne; Sharniece Williams; Sharonda Carter; Shatim Jones; Sheila Robinson; Sidney C. Williams; Simon Linen; sistahealer.com; SoundCrafters; Steven Hudson; T. C. Bullock; T. Shaka Troxler; Taj R Wilson; Tall Alston; Tania Williams; Tanya Washington; Tauhid Shaka Troxler; Tavius Dues Troxler; Techsista Media Share & Distribution; Teri Davis; Terrell Wright; Terrin Jackson; Terry L. Day; The Good Kid II; Theresa Brunson; Thomas Burt; Tito Alston; Toka Waters; Tony Carter Sr. from 143rd St.; Tonya Blount; Tonya D. Johnson; Tonya Manning; Torrie Mitchell; Tracy Owens; Travis Earl Livingstone; Tray Boogie 122nd; Tremain Smith; Tyree Allen; Veronica Gates; Virginia Lambert-Barber; Walter G. Fuller; Walter L. Stevens; Walter R. Paige; Wendy M. Eatherton; Wendy Tomlinson; West Coast Black Television Network; Yasmin Coleman; Yu-Hsuan Yeh; Yvonne Galarza-Fludd

Harlem Godfather:
The Rap on my Husband, Ellsworth "Bumpy" Johnson

Foreword by Shannon Holmes

Underworld organized crime figures from other ethnic groups have long been held in high esteem for their criminal exploits; evidence of which can be seen throughout every media outlet, from magazines, books to film. These criminals are well documented throughout the annals of history.

Hollywood has especially taken up position to glamorize and romanticize their life stories, making a handsome profit in the process. Movies depicting these Caucasian criminals, many of which like *The Godfather*, are considered American cinematic classics. They live on long after the person in question has passed away, later to be discovered by other unsuspecting generation after generation. Even today, urban youths have taken such a liking to the criminal lore that even some rappers and producers have adopted their monikers in part or in whole, i.e. Irv Gotti, as an alias. It is rare if ever that such an honor is bestowed on an African American gangster.

But if ever there was a black criminal who deserves that tribute, then that person would be Ellsworth "Bumpy" Johnson. Before there was a Nicky Barnes, Guy Fisher, Freddie Meyers, or even modern day drug lords like Alpo and Rich Porter there was Bumpy Johnson, 'The Harlem Godfather.'

Nowadays the streets of Harlem languish in a state of uncertainty; with the drug game in shambles, there is no clear cut leader on the streets. There is no organization that excerpts total control. Once upon a time ago there was. Bumpy Johnson and his cohorts ruled black Harlem with an iron fist. Nothing illegal happened unless he gave the word. He was 'the man' before my generation knew who or what the man was. Bumpy was a man amongst men. He was a true stand up guy, who took on the upper echelons of the mafia, and won.

'Way back when,' America was looked upon by foreigners as the land of opportunity. But here, at home, in the United States the Black man couldn't even find decent work to feed his family. Foreigners routinely came from across seas and took all the best jobs, even in the criminal realm. Time and time again, the Black man was underestimated and overlooked. Conditions such as these spurred many law abiding black men to enter into a life of crime. They merely took the bitter fruit – the lemons -- that the corrupt political infrastructure gave them, and made sweet lemonade. From the undercarriage of society the have-nots were born. From humble beginnings came a true American Gangster. When the streets of New York were ripe for the taking, Bumpy Johnson carved out his own piece of the American dream. This man was larger than life.

In between these pages lie the answers to the mystery surrounding his life. See why Bumpy Johnson was reviled by some, loved by many, but respected by all.

Chapter One – Godfather of Harlem

It wasn't unusual for a gunshot victim to be wheeled into the operating room of Sydenham Hospital in Harlem in 1952. Especially in the wee hours of the morning when club hoppers with too much to drink took their nine-to-five frustrations out on whoever was available.

But this was no usual gunshot victim. This was my husband, Ellsworth "Bumpy" Johnson.

The man who, according to legend, almost single-handedly fought the infamous Jewish hoodlum Dutch Schultz when that notorious madman tried to take over the Harlem numbers rackets. The man who was as well-known for his charity to children as for his deadly temper when he was crossed by other gangsters. The man who was the undisputed King of the Harlem Underworld. The man to whom I'd been married only three years. And from the looks of things, the 45-year-old man who was about to take his last breath.

"Bumpy," Detective Philip Klieger yelled as he trotted alongside the gurney towing the bloodied half-conscious man, "You know you're not going to make it. Tell me who shot you so we can bring him to justice."

But see, my husband lived by the gangster code. Bumpy opened his eyes and momentarily focused on the detective, and his slackened lips curled into a snarl. "A man can only die once, and dead men make no excuses," he managed to get out before falling into full unconsciousness.

"Lord," screamed a heavily-painted woman with a crimson red dress two sizes too tight and about six inches too short. "That boy done killed Bumpy."

'That boy, ' I found out later, was 31-year-old Everett Loving; also known as Robert "Hawk" Hawkins, a brash young gambler from Ashville, North Carolina who fancied himself a pimp, and was considered simply a joke by the Harlem hustlers.

"The kid was nothing but a punk," legendary cardsharp Finley Hoskins would say later. "No one ever paid him no mind. No one ever had no reason to."

But in June 1952 the tall dark-skinned Hawk was determined to make someone take him seriously. He desperately wanted to be accepted by the Harlem hustlers whose number he so urgently wanted to join. He wanted to impress them. He needed to make a name for himself.

For those of you who don't know, New York bars and clubs are open until 4 a.m., but for serious partiers, that's still way too early to go home. These folks would then head for the illegally run After-Hour joints. True, there were some joints that you had to knock on the door and say "Joe, sent me," or give some kind of password, but many others operated in plain view. As long as the owners made their weekly donations to the police no one bothered them. The Vets Club, which was located at 122nd Street and St. Nicholas Avenue, was owned by John Levy – the abusive boyfriend/manager of jazz great Billie Holiday, and Vincent Nelson – one of the most successful pimps in Harlem. By 3 a.m. the joint would be jumping and the folks would be stomping. There was always a good time and a good crowd at The Vets.

On this particular night, jazz great Sarah Vaughn was there sipping champagne, along with the Brown Twins – Vivian and Hibbie -- a popular dance duo. The gorgeous vamp Margherite Chapman, who would later marry baseball slugger Willie Mays (she was a lot older than him, but she lied to him about her age.) was there also, along with a couple of black Hollywood starlets who wished they looked as good as Margherite, and R&B diva Dinah Washington was holding court to her usual entourage of ten or twelve.

It was about 5:30 a.m. when the already half-drunk, Hawk sauntered over to the bar and ordered a scotch, then proceeded to loudly talk about his take for the night – the trick money his "bitches" had turned over to him after a night of whoring.

"Man, why don't you cool out? Can't you see there's ladies in here? Show some respect," Bumpy said irritably as he clinked the ice in his watered down glass of ginger ale. As bad as Bumpy was, he didn't like men cursing around women they didn't know.

To be honest, I don't believe Hawk even looked up to see that it was Bumpy, because he would have been stupid to say what he said next. "Nigger, who the fuck is you to tell me to cool out?" he yelled in his heavy southern accent.

Bumpy looked him up and down and then said quietly, "I'm about to be your worst nightmare. Now carry your behind outta here before someone has to carry you out."

This time Hawk did look up before saying anything else, and that's when he realized who it was he'd been addressing. Intoxicated, but not stupid, Hawk turned to leave but stumbled over a chair on the way out. Someone snickered and Hawk angrily whirled around to say something, but Bumpy looked at him with an icy stare and said, "You still here?"

Ego bruised, Hawk left. Bumpy bought a round a drinks for the ladies as an apology for the rudeness of the younger man, and the merriment continued as it had been before the intrusion.

An hour later most of the party-goers were gone, and my husband was standing at the bar talking to the bartender, and the club owners John Levy and Vincent Nelson when he suddenly felt a nudge on his shoulder and turned around. Hawk, had topped off the scotch he'd already imbibed with cheap wine, and armed with liquid courage and a borrowed revolver he had come back to seek his revenge.

"What you got to say now, nigger?" he screamed as he shakily pointed the gun at Bumpy's head. "You so fucking bad, what you gotta say now?"

Bumpy was out on bail and carried no knife or gun, and because he was backed up against the bar, there was no way he could escape.

"Man, why don't you go home and sleep it off?" Bumpy said calmly as he stretched his hand out behind him, hoping to grasp something on the bar that he could use as a weapon. "You were wrong and you got called out on it. It's over now."

"Ain't shit over," Hawk yelled as he stepped back and tightened his finger on the trigger to take his shot. But just then Bumpy managed to grab a potted plant and smashed it into the side of Hawk's face. It was enough to throw off Hawk's aim, and the bullet meant for Bumpy's head slammed into the right side of his chest instead, and two more shots barreled into his stomach. Bumpy slumped to the floor – eyes closed -- and for a moment Hawk stood over him as if just realizing what he'd done. But when Bumpy reopened his eyes, and Hawk realized he was still alive, Hawk flew out the door.

"Bumpy, are you alright?" the bartender asked as he, Vince, and Levy rushed over to the fallen man.

"I'm fine," Bumpy said in a weak and shaky voice. "Just help me to my feet."

Levy and the bartender half-carried Bumpy to Vince's car, and they sped off to Sydenham Hospital on 124th Street and Manhattan Avenue. .

As Vince helped Bumpy up the stairs another gambler and pimp, Gershwin Miles, called from across the street. "Bumpy is that you? You alright, man?"

"Naw, man. I've been shot," Bumpy managed to yell back to his friend.

No lie, it seemed like all of Harlem must have been listening because within ten minutes the hospital was filled with people trying to see what had happened to Bumpy.

I was home asleep when Vincent called me to tell me what had happened. I almost had a heart attack right there in bed when he said, "Mayme, you'd better hurry. The doctors aren't sure he's going to make it."

Bumpy and I had only been married three years, and while I knew there was always a chance he'd get hurt in his line of work, somehow it never occurred to me that he might be killed and I would be a widow. Call me naïve. I wanted to break down in tears, but I didn't have time. My man was in trouble, and I had to get to him as soon as possible – I couldn't waste any time going into hysterics. We were living at 2 West 120th Street on the third floor at the time, and Walter Clark – who owned the then famous but now defunct Uncle Walter's Sausage – lived on the sixth floor. I hurriedly called his wife, Willa Mae, and asked her to rush downstairs to take care of Bumpy's 2-year-old granddaughter, Margaret, then I got dressed and was downstairs in less than five minutes. I hadn't thought about how I would get to the hospital, but I needn't have worried, Vince was already outside the building in his long black Cadillac. He must have sped through every single red light to make it there that fast. I hopped in the car, and it seemed it was only a few minutes later that we were at Sydenham Hospital.

We pulled up in front of the hospital and I believe I actually jumped out the car before Vince even had a chance to put the car in park. As I ran up the steps I heard someone call out, "Mayme! Let him know I'm here but I can't come in." I looked around and saw a dope dealer named George Iser peeking out from the bushes. "There's cops in there and I still got warrants on me," he explained, "But I just wanna make sure Bumpy's okay. Let him know I'm out here."

I quickly nodded before walking into the hospital. The lobby was packed with people; it seemed like hundreds of people. There were people there in their night clubbing clothes, men there with pants pulled on over their pajamas, women with coats thrown over their nightgowns, and detectives, doctors and nurses all over the place. It was just ridiculous. I actually had to push my way in.

Hoss Steele, Junie Byrd, Finley Hoskins, Steve Mitchell, John Levy and Georgie Rose – all of whom had known Bumpy from when he first moved to Harlem as a teenager – were already there. Steve gave a yell when he saw me, and he and Vince shoved people out the way to get me to the doctor so I could sign the papers for them to operate. It was only then that I saw Bumpy, as they were wheeling him into the operating room. There were two detectives running alongside the gurney, and I had to push them aside to get to my husband. I almost fainted when I looked at him – his beautiful chocolate complexion was an ashen gray, and his beautiful almond-shaped brown eyes were glazed, and only half-open. I fought back a sob as I reached for his hand and gave a reassuring squeeze. To my delight he was able to give a weak squeeze back in return. It restrengthened me.

"Will you get the hell out of here?" I screamed at the detectives who now had the nerve to try and push me out the way to continue questioning Bumpy.

"You heard, Mrs. Johnson," I heard a voice behind me say. "Please get out the way so we can get this man into the operating room." I turned around and saw Dr. Harold Wardrow, a well-known black surgeon, standing there with a scowl on his face.

The operation took six hours, and when it was over Dr. Wardrow came over and told me, "Mrs. Johnson, had the bullet in his chest been one one-tenth of an inch to the left it would have pierced his heart and we wouldn't be here speaking now because your husband would be dead. And to be honest, we've done all we can, but it'll still be touch and go for the next few days. I suggest that you pray for your husband's survival."

I immediately sank to my knees there in the hospital waiting room, clasped my hands together, and looked up toward heaven.

"Dear Lord," I said. "I know that my husband hasn't always been the most upright citizen, but he's always been an upright man. And I love him very much, Dear Lord. Please don't take Bumpy away from me."

I stayed on my knees for another fifteen minutes sending up prayer after prayer. When I got up and turned to face Hoss Steele, Junie Byrd, Vince Nelson, John Levy, Ritchie Williams and George Rose I was surprised and touched to see tears in their eyes – these men were considered to be some of the toughest men in Harlem, and they were on the verge of breaking down with emotion. Suddenly Steve cleared his throat and spoke. "Look, the doctors done all they could, and

Mayme got the God thing in hand, let's go get out in the street and kill that punk motherfucka Hawk."

Without another word they all walked out the hospital and got in their cars and sped off. They never did find Hawk, though. We found out later that once he ran out the Vets Club he got in the car and drove to Albany, New York and hid out there before finally high-tailing it back to North Carolina.

Bumpy's operation was on Monday, but by the time the Amsterdam News – a well-known African-American newspaper in New York which still operates today – hit the stands on Thursday, he was still in a coma. Their headlines screamed *"Bumpy Johnson Near Death After Being Shot During After Hours Spot Brawl."*

The nuns at the Sisters of Handmaid of Mary lit candles and prayed for his recovery. Harlem luminaries called the hospital every hour to check on his prognosis. And Harlem sporting men and women gathered together in their familiar haunts while they awaited word on the condition of their unofficial leader.

Al Capone may have ruled Chicago. Lucky Luciano may have run most of New York City. But, when it came to Harlem, the man in charge was my man, Bumpy Johnson.

He was called an old-fashioned gentleman. He was called a pimp. A philanthropist and a thief. A scholar and a thug. A man who admonished children to stay in school, and a man who District Attorney William O'Brien once said was the most dangerous man in New York.

Bumpy was a man whose contradictions are still the root of many an argument in Harlem. But there is one thing on which everybody could agree – in his lifetime, Ellsworth "Bumpy" Johnson was "the man" in Harlem.

If you wanted to do anything in Harlem, anything at all, you'd better stop and see Bumpy because he ran the place. Want to open a number spot on the Avenue? Go see Bumpy. Thinking about converting your brownstone into a speakeasy? Check with Bumpy first.

The police knew it – they came to him to negotiate peace between young street gangs. The politicians knew it – they counted on him to deliver votes on Election Day. Even the Italian and Jewish syndicate knew it, although they had to find out the hard way. When they decided to move on the Harlem numbers racket, Bumpy, only 25 at the time, sprang into action. With only a handful of loyal men behind him, Bumpy waged a successful guerilla war, forcing the white mobsters to finally come to terms with "that crazy nigger." Even Lucky Luciano, the head of organized crime in New York City, publicly gave Bumpy his due – Black Harlem only recognized one crime boss, and that was Bumpy Johnson.

Bumpy was willing to use his fists and his guns to get what he wanted, but he was just as willing to use his money to help Harlemites in need.

If he saw a family's furniture being moved out in the street because they couldn't pay the landlord –not an uncommon sight in Depression-era Harlem – he would reach into his pocket and peel off a few large bills from the huge wad he carried, and hand it to the evictors to pay off the back rent.

Each year Bumpy personally threw huge Christmas parties at the Rhythm Club on Seventh Avenue and spent thousands of dollars on those economically-deprived children Santa Claus always seemed to forget.

Yes, Bumpy may have been a criminal, but he was a criminal with a social conscience. In this community that felt exploited and abused by both the government and the white criminal element, Bumpy was an underworld leader who took from the people, but at least gave something back.

Me? I don't know. I knew who and what Bumpy was when I met him, and I never did intend to fall in love with him, but I did. And I fell hard.

I was born in North Carolina, not far from Ashville. My parents were sharecroppers, and we were poor. Very poor. And I knew from a very early age that I didn't like being poor. And people started telling me, at a very early age, that with my looks I wouldn't have to be poor long. I was what they called light, bright, and damn near white, with straight light-brown hair that hung down my back. By the time I was 14 men were already beginning to notice me. Problem was, there in the backwoods of North Carolina, the men who were noticing me weren't about anything, and had no prospect of ever being about anything. I wasn't what you called a "bad girl," but I was certainly looking for a way out of North Carolina and away from the smell of wet tobacco. I had a series of "male callers," and like many young girls getting a lot of male attention, I made some mistakes. One of them resulted in me being a single mother at age 20. And let me tell you, being a single mother in 1934 was a lot different than being a single mother in 2004. My family was scandalized, and people would whisper and point, and discourage their young daughters being around because I was "fast." It was hard, but I swallowed their crap, but never my pride, and kept my head high. I think that's when I learned to just ignore what people said and to just keep on keeping on. It served me well later on in life.

In 1938 my father died, and we had to borrow money to bury him since he didn't have life insurance. I was working as a live-in domestic in Durham at the time, making four dollars a week. My sister, Lucille, lived in New York City, and she encouraged me to come up North because I could make more money, which I could then send home to the family to help pay the burial debt. So I left my daughter, Ruthie, with my mother and headed to Harlem.

The first job I got was as a ladies maid for a white woman named Mildred Lapkin. I didn't stay there long, though. One of the domestics who lived in the building next door said, "Girl, you're way too good looking to be doing some one's laundry. You better use your looks to get you a job to make some real money. Or better yet, get you a man who got some real money and willing to give you some." I didn't have to think it about two minutes before I knew she was right. I liked to stay dressed well, and go out and have a good time. The eight dollars a week I got working for the Lapkin household didn't go far, especially since I was sending most of that home to my mother to help pay bills.

It wasn't long before I landed a real cushy job as hostess at Hagar's Barbecue. Hagar's was right off the Harlem River Speedway, near 180th Street, and was owned by actress/singer Ethel Waters. She named it after the character "Hagar" she played in the celebrated Broadway play, Mamba's Daughters in 1939. In 1940 when I got the job at Hagar's, Ethel was one of the highest paid black actresses in Hollywood. She starred in the all black musical revue, Cabin in the Sky, and also played the grandmother in the movie Pinky; which was about a black woman passing for white; and she also had a nightclub act and an evening radio show. Ethel was famous, and rich, but could be a real bitch, if you don't mind my saying. She wasn't that much to look at, and was jealous as hell of anyone who was; and she really hated on people who had talent that might rival hers. She used to badmouth people like Sarah

24

Vaughn, saying she could sing circles around that girl. And she really hated on Lena Horne, especially when Lena got the lead part in the 1943 movie Stormy Weather with Bill "Bojangles" Robinson. Ethel swore she was the one who made the song Stormy Weather famous when she sang it at the Cotton Club back in the early 1930s, and Lena couldn't do the song justice. They say she gave Lena pure hell when they starred together in Cabin in the Sky because she thought the crew was paying too much attention to her. A lot of people in show business respected Ethel Waters, but they didn't like her.

And not too many people at the restaurant liked her either. She was the boss, and she wanted everyone to know it. Everyone at Hagar's was afraid of her, and jumped whenever they heard her voice, including her husband, Eddie Mallory. Eddie -- who was about ten years younger than Ethel -- used to have quite a name himself back in the thirties as a trumpet player and band leader, but you'd never know it the way Ethel talked to him. He said he didn't mind, though, as long as she paid the bills. And boy did she pay some bills keeping that man dressed! Whew! Eddie was always sharp. And always in brand new sporty cars which he used to escort beautiful young girls around whenever Ethel was out of town, which was quite often because of her career.

I'm not going to lie and say that Ethel was ever particularly mean to me, but I didn't like her because of the way she treated everyone else. Maybe that's why I went along with the bartenders' scheme to steal from her club every night. Or maybe it was simply because, like I said earlier, I liked having money.

I was making three dollars a week salary at Hagar's, but I was actually bringing home something close to sixty dollars a week because I earned about twelve dollars a night in tips. Believe me, sixty dollars a

25

week was crazy money back in the early forties! I was able to send my mother thirty or forty dollars a week and still have enough to dress nice and go out and have a good time. But when the bartender approached me with his little scheme, I started making even more money. The scheme was simple, if a customer gave me a five to get him a drink from the bar, I'd order the drink, hand the bartender the money, and he would hand me back change for a twenty. I'd give the customer back his correct change and pocket the rest. The bartender and I would then split our take at the end of our shift. We did this for years and never got caught. The weeks that bartender and I worked the same shifts I was able to bring home about $200 a week instead of sixty. Now I wasn't only able to buy nice dresses, I was able to buy them at some of the nicer downtown boutiques. I was also able to afford to move from Harlem into a nice little apartment at 86th Street and Central Park West. The landlord and all the other tenants thought I was white, and I didn't tell them any different. I was young, and I was enjoying myself. You're supposed to do that when you're young. I thought that then, and I still think so now.

I went out a lot during that time. Men were always asking me out, and I often went. I wasn't going to bed with them, but I did let them take me out and show me a good time. Nothing wrong with that. And I was always most attracted to men who had money. I always said you don't need a man who doesn't have money because you can do bad by yourself.

One guy I was really attracted to, though, was John Levy. I knew his sister, Gert, and she introduced us. This was about 1945. He used to come into Hagar's all the time, and ask me out. I was kind of leery at first, because I'd heard his reputation as a ladies man, but after awhile I let my guard down and went out with him. John was a good looking man, and such a sweet talker, and he showed me such a good time – before I knew it we were at his house, and I was sitting on the bed with my shoes off. I knew what was coming next, but I didn't care. I was really feeling John Levy. That is until suddenly someone started banging on his door screaming in a high-pitched female voice, "John, you no good nigger. I know you got some woman in there! You got me out whoring in the street and your no good-ass is cheating on me with some bitch."

Well, John hurried up and hustled me into a closet, and pleaded for the woman on the other side of the door to go away, saying he was just in there by himself trying to get some sleep. She finally left, after about a half-hour, and he let me out the closet. I didn't say a word to him. I politely put on my shoes, picked up my pocketbook, and I caught a cab home. I didn't want anything else to do with John Levy. He might have been good looking and a sweet talker, but no man was worth fighting over in my opinion. Besides, from what I could gather from the things being said by the woman banging on the door, John was a man who took money from women. Hell, he'd want to pimp me and I'd want to pimp him. Wasn't going to work. And – I found out later – if John didn't get what he wanted from a woman fast enough, he'd beat the hell out her. He hooked up with blues great Billie Holiday in the late 40's while she was still married to Jimmy Monroe, and it was a shame the way he treated that poor woman. He used to beat her right out there on the street, on Seventh Avenue. It was she who put up most of the bankroll for him to open the Vets Club. And years later, I can remember him bringing her to a party Bumpy and I had after we moved into the Lenox Terrace. She was all bruised, and looked like she was crying, and John – bold as day – said "Bumpy, come here. I got something to show you." He pulled out a pair of her exquisite and expensive gold-encrusted jade earrings from his pocket and offered to sell them to Bumpy right in front of everybody. Billie didn't say anything, she just averted her eyes in shame.

Bumpy was disgusted – John was his boy from way back, but Bumpy liked Billie and didn't think John had to embarrass her like that, selling her jewelry at a party right in front of her. Bumpy pulled out fifty dollars and gave it to John, then snatched the earrings out his hand. I think he did it so John wouldn't go around hawking it to other people at the party and shame poor Billie even more. After the party Bumpy gave me the earrings and said he never wanted to see them again. I still have those earrings. John was a real bastard. That woman banging on the door when she did back in 1945 might have been the best thing that happened to me.

By 1946 I had enough of Hagar's. It was true I was making good money, but I wasn't finding any good men. I decided to try my luck downtown, and I landed a job as hostess at a restaurant called King of the Sea at 53rd Street and Third Avenue. I started dating a couple of white men, but I wasn't into anything serious.

Then one April evening in 1948 I went uptown to eat at Frasier's Restaurant at 122nd and Seventh, because I had a taste for some good chicken, and everyone knew that Frasier's had the best food in Harlem. I had just ordered my food when this good-looking dark-skinned man walked in and took a seat. He was smiling and laughing, and told Mona Frasier that he'd just gotten arrested. I thought that was strange that someone would think it funny that they were arrested, so I listened more intently. He said that he was collecting numbers on 135th Street when he noticed a police officer walking his way. He said he didn't know this officer, and he didn't want to take any unnecessary chances, so he threw the brown paper bag with the numbers in the gutter and kept walking.

"But wouldn't you know," he said, "one of the kids who's always hanging around yelled out behind me, 'Mr. Bumpy! You dropped your bag!' I tried to just keep walking, but the kid picked up the bag and chased after me to give it to me. I couldn't even be mad at the boy, cause he was trying to do the right thing. Of course what wound up happening was he got me arrested." Bumpy started cracking up with laughter again, and so did Mona.

And my ears perked up. Bumpy? Was this the infamous Bumpy Johnson who everyone was talking about? I didn't want it to be obvious, so I tried looking at him from the corner of my eyes. For someone who was supposed to be the toughest man in Harlem, he didn't look all that big. He was about 5'8, with a medium build, chocolate complexion and neatly groomed short hair. He had almond-shaped eyes that twinkled when he laughed. He was a good looking man. Not pretty, but very handsome. Add to that the fact that I knew he had money and he was downright gorgeous.

Bumpy had just finished doing a 10-year stint in Dannemora for slicing up a pimp called New York Charlie, so I'd never had the opportunity to meet him. Now was my chance. I pulled my chair a little away from the table, crossed my legs, and waited for him to notice me in my shocking pink sweater and my form fitting black velvet skirt.

I didn't have to wait long.

"Hey, who's that fine young foxy filly?" I heard him ask Mona.

She told him that my name was Mayme something, and I was up from North Carolina and worked as a hostess at the King of the Sea. He told her that he wanted to buy me a drink, and Mona came up and told me that Bumpy wanted to treat me to a drink. I turned and flashed him a smile, then told Mona to tell him that I didn't drink. Well, he was at my table in just a few seconds insisting that his day just wouldn't be complete if he couldn't persuade me to just have one little drink on him. I gave a big sigh, and said if it meant that much to him, perhaps I'd have a blackberry brandy.

He smiled, and asked if he could join me at my table. I gave a half-smile, and a slight shrug. That was all the encouragement Bumpy needed. He sat down and proceeded to tell me all about him (I pretended I'd never heard of him), learned everything he could about me (I was careful to leave out anything I thought might turn him off), and then he went on to tell me his views on all the current events of the time. I was impressed. This was a really smart man.

Two hours had passed, and we decided to leave the restaurant and go to the movies. It was raining, but we drove to the Strand, which was a huge theater house on Broadway between 48th and 49th Streets. Back in the early 1900s it was a vaudeville stage, but in 1948 it was a first run movie theater so I don't know why it was playing *To Be or Not to Be,* which was first released in 1942, but it was. I'd seen the movie before, but I didn't tell Bumpy. And since it was a good movie I didn't mind seeing it again. I always did like the star, Carole Lombard. She was the wife of movie king Clark Gable, and had died in an airplane crash in a few months before the movie was released. Afterward we went to the apartment he was staying in on 149th Street and Broadway. I couldn't very well take him to my apartment, because all my neighbors thought I was white, remember? And there was no way Bumpy was passing for white.

I figured I'd go upstairs with him to his apartment, he would try to get me in bed, and I would play hard to get and go home, making him want me all the more. To my surprise, Bumpy never made a pass. We stayed up all night talking. I don't think I'd ever done that with a man before. I was intrigued. And he made me laugh. He was doing impersonations, and serenading me with the song *"It Had to Be You,"* which was featured in the film Casablanca. The Ink Spots had just sung the song on the Jack Benny Radio Show a few days earlier, and Bumpy was doing their version. And he had me cracking up with laughter. Oh, Bumpy was a man of many talents, but singing wasn't one of them. He didn't care though; he was just hamming it up. Although I'd just met him that night I was seeing a side of Bumpy that few people saw, and I was enjoying the hell out of it.

We started going out on a regular basis, going to boxing matches, concerts, and night clubs. That's when I found out that while Bumpy couldn't sing he could dance his butt off. In fact, he actually won a couple of Charleston contests! He introduced me to his childhood friends, Nat Pettigrew, Hoss Steele, Ritchie Williams, Steve Mitchell, Junie Byrd, Six-n-Eight (I never did learn his real name. They called him Six-n-Eight because he liked to shoot craps and those were his favorite points), Georgie Rose, and Finley Hoskins.

Before long I was known as Bumpy's girl. It was a good title to possess. It meant I could get in anywhere I wanted to go, I was treated as queen wherever I went, and I was showered with gifts and jewelry on a steady basis. It also meant that I was constantly accosted by other women who were in love with Bumpy and wanted me out of the way. At first I was upset, but then I pretty much learned to ignore them. Like Bumpy said, they wouldn't even be stepping to me if they didn't realize that I was the one real woman in his life. And hell if I was going to let them back me away from a man who treated me as good as Bumpy treated me. Forget downtown boutiques, I was now buying my clothes from Bloomingdale, Saks Fifth Avenue, and even had quite a few tailor-made outfits. I did mention that I like to dress well, right?

As I stated earlier, Bumpy and I met in April 1948. In October that year we were driving past 116th and St. Nicholas Avenue in his Cadillac when he suddenly turned to me and said, "Mayme, I think you and I should go ahead and get married."

I was stunned, but I kept my composure. I said simply, "Is that right?"

He said, "Yes, that's right," and kept on driving.

We were married in a civil ceremony just two weeks later.

I would be a liar if I said I married Bumpy out of love. I would be an even bigger liar if I said I didn't fall madly in love with the man. Don't ask me how, don't ask me why. I can just tell you that one day, about a month after we married, I woke up and looked at him sleeping next to me. Tears filled my eyes, and it suddenly hit me. 'God, I love this man.' I leaned over and kissed him, and he opened his eyes and asked me what that was for. I told him it was because I loved him. He just grinned and pulled me down under him. It was the best lovemaking I'd ever had in my life. And after that, that was it. There would never be another man for me.

And so I stayed and prayed in that hospital room back in 1952, convinced that I'd not be able to go on without him. And, thank the Lord, Bumpy finally opened his eyes five days after the operation. I was there asleep in his room when I heard him kind of grunting. I slowly got up and stood over his bed. He opened his eyes, and it looked as if he were having a hard time focusing for a moment, but when he saw me looking down at him he gave a weak smile, then started humming *"It Had to Be You."* I began crying, and just started hugging him so hard the nurses had to rush in and pry me loose.

The next few days were a blur of activity. There were so many people coming in to visit Bumpy, and his room was always full of flowers. Nurses were doing their best to work on the floor Bumpy was on, because they all wanted to be around him. He was a real charmer, and he turned on his charm with the nurses in the same way he would turn it on with the Black entertainers whom liked to hang out with him. The nurses would stop by his room whenever they got a chance, just to talk. He would ask about how their children were doing in school, or how their parents were making out, and he'd actually listened to the answers. Bumpy was talented that way. When he was talking to you he really gave the impression he really cared. And of course the nurses loved working on Bumpy's floor because they got to meet all of these famous people they'd only heard or read about before. People like Billy Daniels, Sugar Ray Robinson, Billie Holiday, Sarah Vaughn, and Joe Louis all stopped by. Even better were the tips that they received from some of the white visitors from the East Side of Harlem.

"Hey, you make sure you take good care of our pal," the smiling white men would say in their thick New York Italian accents as they slipped $50 and $100 bills into their hands. "Get him back on his feet soon."

The nurses would whisper to each other, "It sure is something – those eye-talians coming out to see Bumpy, but it just shows how important he is. Those are Mafia people you know."

If Bumpy was respected by Harlemites for taking on Schultz, he was just as respected for his relationship with the Italian mobsters who had taken over part of Schultz's operations after his death in 1935. There are some people who now scoff and say that Bumpy was a low-level hood, and none of the Mafia bigwigs would have anything to do with him, but it's a fact that mob boss Lucky Luciano sent me a hand carved antique chess set just two years before his fatal heart attack in 1962.

And when Albert Anastasia was gunned down in a Manhattan barbershop in 1957, police searching the notorious Mafioso's apartment found Bumpy Johnson's home telephone number among Anastasia's papers. Bumpy was in prison at the time, but the FBI came knocking on my door on 120th Street, asking what the head of Murder Inc. was doing with our number. I was scared, but I just told them I didn't know.

There's no doubt about it, the Italian mob respected Bumpy Johnson and everything they did in Harlem was cleared by Bumpy. Even if they wanted to rub out an informer or teach someone a lesson, Bumpy had to be notified, and have the opportunity to pick up the hit contract himself if he so chose. Bumpy was the only Negro who dealt with the Italian mob as if he were their equal. Quite a remarkable feat back in the thirties and forties.

But then Bumpy was quite remarkable.

But along with the many things Bumpy was, and the many things Bumpy wasn't, one of the surest things was that he was no snitch. When detectives brought a picture of Hawk to the hospital and asked Bumpy if that was the man who shot him, Bumpy looked at the photo, smiled and said, "Naw, I ain't never seen that man before."

Later he told me there was no way he was going to identify his assailant for the police. "I'm no rat. I'll deal with him myself."

He never got the chance. Hawk was never seen in New York again.

And that, in a way, was okay . . . because Bumpy had more pressing enemies to worry about. You see, as I mentioned earlier, Bumpy was out on bail at the time of the shooting – he'd been indicted two years earlier on heroin trafficking charges.

Bumpy was a gangster, and everyone in Harlem knew it and accepted it. Yes, he was a number banker, yes he provided paid protection, and yes, he busted a few heads (or shot a few people) from time-to-time, but after all . . . he never really bothered anyone who wasn't already in the criminal world, or hurt anyone who didn't deserve it.

But selling heroin? That was different. That was something that people found it much harder to accept or forgive.

Although Bumpy readily admitted all of his other illegal activities he insisted until the day he died, that he had been framed on the drug charges which sent him to Alcatraz.. He had always admonished children to stay in school and stay away from crime. Now he told them, "See what happened to me? This is what can happen to you if you don't stay straight. I never sold dope, but because I have a reputation with the police I'm being framed."

There are many people who, to this day, believe that Bumpy was indeed set-up, and perhaps with good reason. There were two star witnesses who testified against him – one was a paid-informer who lied and told the jury that he himself had never sold drugs. The other star witness once ran numbers for Bumpy, but had turned on him when Bumpy whipped his butt in front of the Theresa Hotel on 125th Street and Seventh Avenue when Bumpy found out he'd been using his number spots to cash bad checks.

Bumpy appealed his conviction all the way to the U. S. Supreme Court, but the Court refused to hear his appeal.

But through all his regrets of his life, and all his lectures to younger generations to study academics and not crime, Bumpy always maintained a sense of humor about his brushes with the law, and the imprisonment he suffered because of them.

Once, in the early 1960s, a friend asked him to speak to a young white teacher who had been assigned to work in Harlem for the first time.

"Don't you think about anything, you'll like it fine here," he soothingly told the nervous woman.

"Now, you're here for the Head Start program, right? It's a great program," he said. "All these things started under President Kennedy. And me, myself . . . I served under President Kennedy."

"You did?" asked the teacher. "Where?"

He flashed the brilliant smile that was his trademark and answered, "Alcatraz."

That was Bumpy. That was my man.

Chapter Two – The Charleston Years

Bumpy was actually born Ellsworth Raymond Johnson on October 31st, 1905 in the Negro section of Charleston, SC. The darker side of the Negro section of Charleston that is – because the city back then wasn't just divided into White and Colored, the Colored section was divided into light-skinned and dark skinned Colored. And the Johnson family definitely belonged in the latter. They were some dark skinned folks, that family.

Though Ellsworth would later say that his father – William Johnson – was a director of the now defunct Negro Federation Bank, in reality the elder Johnson was an ordinary fisherman, and Ellsworth's mother, Margaret Moultrie Johnson, was a domestic worker. They were the nicest people you'd ever want to meet, and both of them were smart, even if they didn't hold fancy jobs. The family was poor, and lived with their seven children – Margaret (called Margie), Priscilla, Pauline, Willie, Mabel, Genevieve, Elease, and Ellsworth – in a small three bedroom house located at 124 Bogard Street. Well respected in the community, the Johnsons were an extremely religious family who attended church regularly.

To make ends meet, Bumpy's mother worked most of the year in Charleston but also traveled to Brooklyn, New York to work for rich white families whom she'd met while they summered in Charleston. As the three eldest girls grew older she would take them with her to New York to work and send money home for the family. Because of this, Bumpy had little memory of his three older sisters since by the time he was one or two they had found full-time employment in

37

New York, though his mother still came home after her seasonal work in the city was done. Bumpy lived year round with his father, along with Willie, Mabel – who although only eight years older than Ellsworth was his main mother figure – and his sister Elease.

When Priscilla turned 17 she met a well-to-do medical student in Brooklyn and was engaged to be married, but died that same year after drinking tainted water. Her body was shipped home for burial.

Bumpy was only about 3-years-old at the time, and didn't remember much of the whole affair. One thing he did remember, though, was being in the kitchen the morning of the burial while the grown-ups were drinking coffee. He asked his mother for a cup, and she told him he was too young, but Margaret said, "Oh, let him have some," and got up and fixed him coffee mixed with so much milk it was almost white, but he was so grateful that he got his way he said he instantly loved her, and announced she was now his favorite sister. That would change for awhile after Bumpy moved to New York, but I'll get to that later.

By all accounts, Bumpy was an extremely intelligent and out-spoken child, and was skipped at least two grades in the segregated two-room public school house he attended in Charleston along with his sister, Elease, who was three years older than him. He later said that his middle-class father sent him to the prominent Avery Institute, which was attended by the children of prominent black families of the day, but that was bunk. I should tell you now, that when it came to education, Bumpy would lie in a minute. I think it was because the Johnsons really put stock into having a good education, and Bumpy was a little ashamed that he never even finished high school. Yes, I know many people heard stories about him attending City University in New York, but Bumpy made all that up, too. But Bumpy was so damn intelligent and smart no one ever challenged him when he said he had a college education.

Anyway, when Bumpy was about ten a crisis befell the Johnson family. From what he told me, his 19-year-old brother, Willie, was accused of killing a white man. This was South Carolina, a state whose residents were known for taking matters in their own hands when it came to blacks accused of even the slightest infractions against whites.

In 1904, two years before Bumpy was born, one of the most atrocious lynchings in South Carolina occurred.

In Berkeley County – only 40 miles away from Charleston – Kitt Bookard, a 21-year-old tenant farmer – went fishing with six white men. On the way home an argument ensued between Bookard and one of the white men who had earlier molested Bookard's younger sister and Bookard threatened to spank the man. When the group returned to town Bookard was promptly arrested for his impudence, and when he could not pay the $5 fine, was thrown into jail.

Later that day a small group of white men went to the jailhouse and demanded that Bookard be released to them. They then took him to the riverside, scalped him, poked out his eyes, cut off his genitals, cut out his tongue, and then tied him (he was reportedly still alive at this point) to a grate and threw him into the river. The crime was so heinous that even South Carolina Governor Duncan Heywood, was sickened when he heard the details – but no one was ever brought to justice for the crime.

In August 1906 – the year of Bumpy's birth – Bob "Snowball" Davis of Greenwood County was accused of attempting to rape a white woman. The man was tracked down after a two-day manhunt, but the vigilantes decided it would be a waste of taxpayer's money to turn him over for trial when they could mete out the proper punishment themselves. Upon hearing this, Governor Heywood drove to the county and pleaded with the mob to let court justice take its natural course, reminding them about the national attention that South Carolina received after the lynching of Bookard, two years before.

"In God's name," the governor begged the ever-growing mob, "do not put another stain on the name of your State."

The leaders of the mob quickly assured Governor Heywood that they had absolutely no intention of torturing Davis in the manner in which Bookard had been tormented; they were simply going to burn him at the stake.

When Heywood insisted, "Let this brute be punished as the law dictates," mob leaders politely informed the democratically elected leader of the state that "there was no earthly chance" that Davis would escape lynching.

After hours of begging, pleading, and even trying to use bribery, the governor gave up and drove home in defeat. He later found out that his appearance in front of the mob might have made some smidgen of difference after all – the mob decided to tie Davis to a tree and shoot him rather than burn him alive at the stake. Again, no one was ever brought to justice for the lynching – even though the governor of the state could have given eyewitness testimony as to some of the participants. That's just how things were in South Carolina back then.

So when Willie came home and told the family about the incident with the white man who he'd been accused of killing, his parents panicked. They knew they had to get him out of town and fast, but had no money to do so. William – with the blessing and urging of his wife – went to the local banker and took a huge mortgage out on their house, and after paying the local authorities a large amount of money to look the other way, used the remaining cash to sneak Willie out of town and send him to live in New York with Margaret and Pauline.

But the mortgage from Willie's escape from Charleston put the Johnsons into such financial straits it forced almost everyone in the family to work overtime – in any capacity they could find – to try to pay off the loan so that they wouldn't lose their home. Shortly afterward Mabel moved to New York to join Margaret and Pauline and also find work so she could earn a steady paycheck and send money home to help out. William started visiting neighboring towns to sell his catch of the day, and his wife worked herself into bad health trying to save the house. Everyone did their share. Everyone, that is, except Willie.

Bumpy and Elease were the only ones left home, and they saw their parents become old and sick trying to pay off that mortgage; and Willie, the one who caused the problem, seemed to be the only one who didn't care. Willie got bored shortly after he arrived in New York and joined the Merchant Marines, but never bothered to send a dime home to help out, Bumpy told me later. Bumpy never forgave him for that.

But three years later, it was Bumpy who had to be put on a train heading up north.

Even as a young teenager, the quick-witted, intelligent, and oh so very charming Bumpy Johnson was already a ladies man, and not only were the colored girls (dark-skinned and light) enamored with him, so were some of the young white girls in Charleston, which worried the Johnson family. Especially since Bumpy had already shown signs of a quick temper, and

41

they knew if he was ever confronted by whites he wouldn't be inclined to hold his tongue. Even as young boy, Bumpy was what we used to call a "race man." Someone who spoke out about the injustices heaped upon the black man. And there were plenty of injustices to speak out about.

On April 6, 1917, the United States entered World War I, and on May 18th of that year Congress approved the Selective Service Act, authorizing the draft of all men between the ages of 20 and 30. More than 700,000 African-American men volunteered for the draft the very next day. Ultimately more than two million African-Americans registered, and about 100,000 African-American men were sent to France. Though Army policy at the time relegated most of those men to non-combative situations, about 40,000 of these men actually saw action. While the African-American soldiers were welcomed by the French, they were unable to shrug off the yoke of racism placed upon them by the U. S. Army brass. The Army's feeling was that blacks couldn't fight, and would run away placing their white comrades in even more danger; or that blacks would become subversives for the enemy since they were an "oppressed minority." The brass held onto these beliefs even in the face of extraordinary proof to the contrary. For instance, an African-American, Eugene Jacques Bullard, had joined the French Foreign Legion in 1915, and when the war broke out in France he voluntarily transferred to the French Air Service and flew in more than 20 combat missions, earning the ominous nickname "The Black Swallow of Death." Yet despite this outstanding record, Bullard was never allowed to fly for the United States after it entered the war. And the all black 369th Infantry Regiment was dubbed "The Hellfighters" (they were later known as the Harlem Hellfighters) because in 191 days at the front they never had any men captured or lost any ground. The French gratefully awarded the regiment the Croix de Guerre, but the U. S. Army barely took notice of their achievements.

The Germans, quick to pick up on the racial tension inside the U.S. troops, would regularly fly over black troops and drop propaganda leaflets discouraging them from fighting for a country that did not treat them fairly. One such leaflet read: "To carry a gun in this service is not an honor but a shame. Throw it away and come over to the German lines. You will find friends who will help you." Their urgings were ignored.

When the Armistice was signed in 1918, and black soldiers were sent home, they were dismayed, but not shocked, to find that nothing had changed in their absence. But they were now not as willing to silently suffer their slights. When told they were scheduled to march in the back of the victory parade arranged by St. Joseph, Missouri for returning troops, black soldiers refused to participate at all, stating publicly that it was incompatible with the principles of democracy for which they had fought.

Their uppity-ness did not sit well, however, with Southern whites. In 1919, in a period James Weldon Johnson – composer of the "Negro National Anthem – later called the "Red Summer," cities throughout the nation including Charleston; Chicago; Elaine, AR; Knoxville, TN and Washington D.C. were rocked by racial riots. News reports of the day indicated that all of the uprisings were instigated by whites. Hundreds of blacks were severely wounded, and 75 were outright lynched – ten of these were black veterans.

In most of the melees blacks were no more than hapless victims, but in Washington D.C. they armed themselves and fought back. The New York Times denounced the black militancy and lamented: "There had been no trouble with the Negro before the war when most admitted the superiority of the white race."

Jamaican poet Claude McKay penned his famous poem "If We Must Die" in response to the 1919 riots:

> *If we must die let it not be like hogs*
> *If we must die, let it not be like hogs*
> *Hunted and penned in an inglorious spot*
> *While round us bark the mad and hungry dogs*
> *Making their mock at our accursed lot.*
> *If we must die, O let us nobly die*
> *So that our precious blood may not be shed*
> *In vain; then even the monsters we defy*
> *Shall be constrained to honor us though dead!*
> *O kinsmen we must meet the common foe!*
> *Though far outnumbered let us show us brave*
> *And for their thousand blows deal one deathblow!*
> *What though before us lies the open grave?*
> *Like men we'll face the murderous, cowardly pack*
> *Pressed to the wall, dying, but fighting back!*

The poem became a favorite of Bumpy's, and though the Johnson family had managed to keep the already belligerent Bumpy from participating in the Charleston riots they realized he wouldn't last long in Charleston if he continued to openly espouse views – especially when he began to openly praise his black brothers in D.C. who had taken a stand against marauding whites. A decision was made that he too had to make the journey to New York, and they sent him to live in Harlem with Mabel who had recently married and was living in a railroad flat on 150th Street and Seventh Avenue.

Chapter Three – From Ellsworth to Bumpy

So many people complain these days that Harlem is no longer black, which is funny to me because Harlem wasn't always black. In fact, there was a time when it was lily white – well except for the colored maids and butlers.

You see, at the turn of the century – the last century that is – Blacks lived in an area called The Tenderloin – the area around West Twenty-third to Fifty-second Street. They shared the area, however, with the Irish and racial tensions were high. In 1863 – after the draft was instituted for the first time – an Irish mob, angry about being forced to fight in the Civil War, rioted and killed hundreds of black men while city officials did nothing. Even after the Civil War riots there were numerous incidents of white brutality against blacks, many involving the police.

Harlem, at the time, was almost solely inhabited by upper middle-class whites. Philip Payton – brother-in-law of James Weldon Johnson, the man who wrote the black national anthem, Lift Every Voice and Sing – was an up and coming real estate investor, and when he heard that a Harlem landlord was upset because the tenants of his building on 134th Street and Fifth Avenue (now the site of The Lenox Terrace) were on a rent strike, he approached the landlord with an incredible idea. Why not let "good" blacks move into some of the vacant apartments in the building? The landlord jumped at the idea, knowing the blacks would willingly pay twice what white tenants were paying.

But only weeks after the first black family moved in, the white families began moving out in droves. It was white flight at its finest! By 1908 or so, blacks were firmly established in Harlem. White

Harlem shop owners at first didn't mind. Many didn't live in the neighborhood themselves, and they hiked up the prices on their wares when blacks moved in, so they were doing quite well. That is until blacks started trying to open up their own businesses. Then the white storeowners started importing Irish thugs from The Tenderloin and Hells Kitchen to come up to Harlem to put the darkies in their place.

But see, blacks had laid claim to Harlem, and they weren't going to give it up without a fight. While the white shop owners imported their thugs from downtown, black Harlem shop owners found men amongst their own community who loved to fight, and saw no reason why they shouldn't make a couple of dollars doing so. These men, which included William "Bub" Hewlett, and Max "Thump" Sheldon, became known as the Harlem Bad Men -- or as the mostly Irish police force in Harlem referred to them, "those crazy niggers." They were fearless men who never walked the streets without a knife, baseball bat or gun in hand, and looked forward to any excuse to use it, whether it be against the Irish thugs who dared to invade Harlem, or the white police who backed them.

Bub was the fiercest of them all, though. Born in Virginia in 1888, the man was about 6'1, broad shouldered, and cocky as he wanted to be. He could be a nice guy at times, but he could also be mean as hell. I met him later in his life, but even then you knew he wasn't the one to be messing with. You knew one blow from one of those big fists of his and you were on your way to meet your maker. One of the things I remember the most about him is how he could eat. He would come home to dinner with Bumpy sometimes to finish talking business, and there was many a time when I saw him devour a whole chicken by himself. I didn't really mind, because I loved to cook, but I started telling

46

Bumpy to let me know ahead of time when Bub was coming over so I had enough to feed the man.

People think they know about Bub because of the film Hoodlum – he was the character played by Clarence Williams, III. I actually got sick to my stomach when I saw how they portrayed Bub in that movie, though. Remember the scene where Dutch Schultz forced Bub to take his leftovers home to feed his family? That was just bull. Bub woulda taken a bullet rather then let himself be humbled like that. Bub was a proud man. A real proud man. And very proud of how he took care of his family. He had four children, and he paid for all of them to get a good education. Two of his sons went on to become doctors, the third a dentist. His daughter –who's still alive – became head of one of the largest adoption agencies in New York – and Bub paid for all of their college and postgraduate educations. Bub had a right to feel proud. The people who made that movie had no right to portray him like a flunky. Yes, it's true he worked for Dutch Schultz for awhile, but he was no damn flunky.

Anyway, I'll get more into that later.

By the time Bumpy got to Harlem in 1919 blacks had won their fight to keep their claim on the community, thanks to men like Bub, and Harlem – was without doubt -- the homeland for blacks in New York City.

Bumpy's family had arranged for him to stay with his sister Mabel who lived on 150th Street near Seventh Avenue. She had married, but her husband was in the army and she lived in a railroad flat with her two daughters. The apartment was crowded and Bumpy had to sleep on the couch, but he had no intention of staying there long. Mabel tried to be as strict with him as she was with her own children. They had to dress and talk a certain way to impress the neighbors, because Mabel was big on impressing the neighbors. The family had little more than two nickels to rub together, but Mabel tried to make believe that they were doing as well as the doctors and lawyers who lived up on Sugar Hill. They barely had enough money to buy groceries or kerosene for heat, but she would strut into the Abyssinia Baptist Church every Sunday wearing a fine dress and hat and sit fanning herself while Rev. Adam Clayton Powell, Sr. made his weekly sermon. And she'd cluck her teeth at the little hooligans running the streets "like heathens with no good upbringing."

It would drive Bumpy crazy, and he would later tell me his plan was to find his favorite sister, Margaret, who had let him have that coffee so many years before. He knew that she loved him dearly, and that she lived alone and that she would welcome him. He also knew that she was doing pretty well. She had a full-time job and attended Pratt Institute at night. There would be plenty of room for him to stay with her. But he was surprised and hurt that Mabel wouldn't tell him where Margaret lived. He argued with Mabel, and begged, but she wouldn't budge. She told him that their parents had decided he should live with her and that's the way it was going to be. Bumpy was bitter, but he had no choice. He would stay with Mabel, but hell if he was going to make believe he liked it.

Bumpy was rather small for his age, but he was tough. But the kids in Harlem didn't see tough, they just saw small. With his small stature and his thick Southern accent he soon became a target for the neighborhood bullies. I heard this story from Bumpy and his friends so many times I know it by heart.

It was the first day of school when he had his first real run-in with them. He was dressed in second-hand blue pants and a neatly starched white shirt and a red bowtie, and had a roll of pennies in his pocket, the lunch money Mabel had given him. He and Mabel had argued that morning, just as they did when she took him to register for high school. You see Bumpy wanted to get a job so he could send money home to help the family pay off the debt caused by Willie's flight, but Mabel wasn't hearing it. She didn't want her neighbors talking about her having a brother who didn't even have an education.

He was only two blocks from the school when he passed six other young teenagers on the corner, shooting dice against a building. Bumpy slowed down to take a look.

"Seven! You crapped out," one teenager with thick coke-bottle glasses shouted as he scooped up the dice with one hand and the money on the sidewalk with the other.

"The hell with that, Finley," a tall stocky dark-skinned yelled. "How you gonna scoop them up before I even seen if I made my point?"

"Don't even try it, Six-n-Eight. I got the dice now," Finley said shaking the dice. "Put your money down on the ground if you're gonna place another bet."

Six-n-Eight dipped into his pocket and came up empty. "Shit! You done cleaned me out. I ain't even got lunch money."

"Yeah? Well that ain't my problem, punk," Finley said nonchalantly. "Now either put some dough on the ground or get out the way so someone else can. Baby needs a new pair of shoes."

"Sheet, Nigga. You ain't got no baby," the largest boy in the crowd said with a sneer. "You ain't even got a girlfriend."

"As long as I got these little beauties in my hand I don't need no damn girl, Nat. Now put up or shut up. I ain't got all day," Finley answered still shaking the dice in his hands.

The boy called Nat shrugged and threw two quarters on the sidewalk, and Finley tossed the dice against the building. "Six," he said peering at them as they fell to the ground. "My point is six."

"Damn, you ain't gonna make no six. That's my lucky point. You ain't making it," Six grumbled. "I need a piece of that action."

"Then put your money where your mouth is, son." Finley said as he scooped up the dice and began shaking them in his hand.

"Let me hold on to a dollar, Fin," Six-n-Eight started pleading.

"What? I look like some damn fool?" Finley said as Bumpy turned to walk away. "I don't gamble against my own money. Now put up or shut up."

"Hey, Six," Bumpy heard someone say. "I know where you can get some money. I bet old country boy over there got some cash."

"Yeah, Junie!," Six-n-Eight said with enthusiasm. He reached out and grabbed Bumpy by the arm. "Hey, you. Country. What you got in your pocket?"

"My hand," Bumpy said quickly. "Why? You got a problem with that?"

"Oh, country boy got some mouth on him," the boy named Junie said with a laugh.

"Well, take your hand outta your pocket and let me see what else is in there," Six-n-Eight said moving in closer to Bumpy.

"Man, you don't want me to take my hand out my pocket," Bumpy said in a calm voice. "Cause if I do I'm gonna smash it against your head."

Finley had been watching silently, still in his gambling crouch, but he suddenly straightened up and held up two-dollar bills in his hand. "I got a deuce that says Six-n-Eight kills that boy. Anybody wanna take the bet?"

"You know what? I'ma go with little Country over here. I got a feeling 'bout him," Nat said.

"That little bitty boy? Six-n-Eight's gonna pulverize him," Junie said rubbing his hands together. "Hey, Six," he called out. "I turned you onto him so I get half of whatever you get offa him, man."

"Believe me, you ain't gonna want half of what he's gonna get if he don't get out my face," Bumpy said.

"Man, Country talking some big time shit!" someone shouted as a crowd began to gather around Bumpy and Six-n-Eight.

Six-n-Eight threw the first punch – a left hook aimed right at Bumpy's chin. Too bad for him it didn't connect. Bumpy was the smaller of the fighters, and the quickest. He easily sidestepped the blow, and Six was thrown off balance. That's when Bumpy finally took his hand out of his pocket, and just as he promised Six was sorry he did. His fist landed smack in the middle of Six's face, and blood spurted over Bumpy's starched white shirt. Six's eyes rolled in the back of his head, and he sunk to his knees – his nose broken.

That's when Bumpy threw his second punch -- a haymaker that exploded against the side of Six's head.

Six still didn't go all the way down, and grabbed Bumpy's pants trying to pull himself up. Bumpy smashed him in the face again, but this time when he connected copper coins spilled onto the sidewalk.

"Oh shit, that country nigga had a roll of pennies in his fist!" someone shouted.

"That's not fair. He's fighting dirty," Finley yelled as he pushed closer to get a better look while Bumpy continued to rain punches on Six trying to get him to release his hold on his trousers.

51

"Ain't no one called a fair one," Nat said rubbing his hands together. "You paying me my two bucks."

"Come on, Six! Get up and kill the punk," Junie yelled.

"Get him, Country!" Nat called out.

Bumpy was finally able to pull away from Six's grasp, and he stepped back and landed a hard kick square between Six's legs. Well, that was the end of that. Six grabbed his balls and fell to the sidewalk. Bumpy pulled his leg back and aimed a kick for Six's head, but a hand grabbed the back of his collar, pulling him back.

"Okay, little nigga. You done won me my money, already, but I can't let you kill my boy here," Nat said, throwing Bumpy against a parked car.

"Fuck you," Bumpy screamed, as he jumped back up and started squaring off against Nat.

"Okay, I got a fin says Nat kills the little nigga," Finley said, pulling a five dollar bill from his pocket.

"Shit, I'll cover that bet," Junie replied excitedly. "That little nigga's crazy. My money's on him."

Nat simply grinned and stepped back from Bumpy. "I ain't fighting you, man. Like I said, you done won me my money. Youse my nigger if you get no bigger. And you'd better be glad there was money riding on this fight, else we all woulda jumped your ass."

Bumpy's lips twisted into a sneer. "And I woulda kicked all of your asses. And I still will!"

Over the years I've heard this same story from Nat, Junie, Finley and Bumpy, and they all would bust out laughing at this point. Like I said, Bumpy was the smallest of the lot, and Nat was a big bruiser even back then. Bumpy swore, though, that had it come to it he would have taken all of them, and I know him well enough to know he probably would have. It didn't come to that, though. Back then the schools had truant officers who roamed the streets looking for kids playing hooky. As luck would have it Junie spotted the truant officer crossing the street and heading in their direction.

"Beat it!" he shouted. "Here comes Mr. Gaines!"

The crowd of boys quickly started scattering in different directions, leaving the injured Six-n-Eight to face the music alone. Bumpy also started running, but wasn't sure where he was heading when he heard Nat call out, "Hey! No! Come on this way or you're gonna get your ass caught!"

Bumpy quickly changed direction and followed behind Nat, Finley and Junie as they ran up Seventh Avenue and then into the hallway of a building on 149th Street.

"You okay, now?" Nat asked as the four of them leaned against one of the buildings to catch their breath when they finally decided they were in the clear.

"I was okay before," Bumpy said. "Shit. Weren't nothing wrong with me."

"What's your name, anyway?" Nat asked.

"Ellsworth."

"Ellsworth? What kinda name is that," Junie asked.

"Mine. What of it?" Bumpy said in a challenging voice.

"Man, calm down, I don't wanna fight. I'm just saying I ain't never hearda no one named Ellsworth," Junie said in a calm voice.

"Damn, if you ain't got a temper on you," Nat said with a laugh. "Yeah, but that's cool." He walked over and stuck his hand out. "How you doing, Ellsworth? My name is Nat, and you can consider me your new best friend. Cause of you I just won my first bet with Finley."

Bumpy looked him up and down for a moment and then slowly shook his hand. "You can call me Bumpy if you want. That's what my friends back home call me."

"Why they call you Bumpy?" Junie asked.

"Cause the little nigga got a funny shaped head," Finley said.

"Don't pay him no mind," Nat said. "He's just mad cause he gots to get up off some money for once in his fucking life." He turned and glared at Finley. "And youse best to pay up, man."

"Double or nothing I roll a seven on my first shot," Finley said, taking the pair of dice out of his pockets and shaking them in his hand.

"Nigga, you betta give me my money," Nat shot back. "I ain't stupid enough to be fucking around with your lucky ass when I'm on the up for once."

Finley reluctantly pulled out two crumpled bills from his pocket and handed them over to Nat. Then he whirled toward Bumpy. "So, you shoot craps?"

"Yeah. I shoot. But I ain't got no money. That roll of pennies was all I had."

"Another broke nigga," Finley said turning away.

"Here." Nat thrust a dollar in Bumpy's hands. "But I'ma tell you, I wouldn't roll against him. Finley always wins."

Bumpy nodded. "You play skin, man?" he asked Finley.

Finley grinned and pulled a deck out his pocket. "Shit. I came out my mama playing Georgia skin."

It didn't take but fifteen minutes for Finley to win Bumpy's dollar and Nat's too. The only thing that saved Junie was the fact that he had already lost all of his money to Finley.

And just like that, the four of them became best friends for the rest of their lives. Later Bumpy would meet Georgie Rose, Ritchie Williams, Steve Mitchell and Obadiah and the crew was complete. Even Six and Bumpy would later become cool, though Bumpy never became as close to him as he did with the others.

Bumpy didn't make it to school that day, and wound up never setting foot in school again. He left Mabel's apartment every morning and hooked up with his friends and they would go out trying to make money hustling pool, shooting craps, or selling newspapers. It wasn't much money, but it was something, and it allowed Bumpy to build up a small stash that he planned to eventually send home. One day, they gathered in a small diner on Seventh Avenue to buy breakfast and the owner of the restaurant, a man named Josh R., told them they could eat for free if they'd sweep the sidewalk outside the shop. The restaurant then became their hangout, and they'd meet there every morning, sweep, eat, and plan the rest of their day. Finley never did any sweeping, but that was okay. The crew made the bulk of their money on the floating crap games that Finley organized. Especially when Finley perfected his "game," and learned how to shoot loaded dice and palm cards.

Soon they started sweeping the sidewalks in front of Harlem businesses to make more money, and that's when Bumpy first met Bub Hewlett. Even though there was no longer any threat from white shop owners and thugs from Hell's Kitchen, Bub and his crew still managed to squeeze money from businesses by providing protection against local thugs. As long as they were paid, proprietors didn't have to worry about their shops being broken into at night, or themselves being robbed when heading home with their daily take.

Even though Bumpy was the newest member of the crew, he was definitely the brains, and it didn't take him long to realize that he, Junie, Nat, Georgie, Ritchie, Steve, Obadiah and Six-n-Eight could make money themselves offering protection to some of the newer shops opening along Lenox and Seventh Avenues.

Well, one fine day Bub heard about a grocery store opening on Seventh Avenue near 148th Street so he drove over to introduce himself to the owner and offer his protection services. To his surprise the owner told him that he was already paying for protection. He then pointed to Bumpy, who was leaning on Bub's black Lincoln, his arms crossed, staring intently at Bub through the store window.

"That little nigger?" Bub asked with a laugh, and not waiting for an answer, he strode out the door to confront the 16-year-old.

"Get up off my car, little nigger," Bub demanded, once outside. "You know who I am?"

"Yeah, I know. You're Bub Hewlett," Bumpy said as he slowly stood up. "Now I'm off your car. So get up off my block."

"Your block?" Bub asked, towering over the then 5 foot 8 Bumpy by about 4 inches. "How the hell is this your block?"

"Cause me and my boys claimed it. At least we claiming this store," Bumpy said in an unwavering voice. "You and your friends got most of the businesses in Harlem already tied up, so now that a new one's opened it's ours."

Bub grinned and gave a slight nod of his head. "Yeah, alright. I understand about youngsters needing to start out on their own. Just as long as they show respect. How about you give me a little piece of your

56

action here and I'll let you take this spot. We'll be partners."

It was Bumpy's turn now to give a slight nod. "Yeah, okay. Me and my boys do our pickups on Sunday mornings. You show up then you get your share, or you tell us where you want us to meet you and we'll bring it to you, and then you can give us our share of your spots, partner."

Bub later said he believed he could have taken Bumpy out with one punch, but he liked "the little nigger's nerve," so he just laughed and drove away, thinking he'd deal with him another day. But it wasn't long before he developed a real liking for Bumpy, who was one of the few people who didn't back down just because Bub raised his voice.

Bumpy's crew also started pulling small burglaries downtown – well, all but Finley. But he was the one made the connect for fences to get rid of the loot, so he always made some money off their escapades. That was Finley, always finding a way to make a dime without getting his hands dirty.

Bumpy was finally making a decent amount of money, but he couldn't figure out a way to send it home to Charleston without Mabel finding out and asking him where he'd gotten the cash. She still thought he was going to school when he left the apartment every morning. But then one day he found an envelope that had Margaret's address lying on the dining room table. He quickly copied the address and the next day he took the subway to Brooklyn to find her.

Bumpy told me he was both nervous and excited as he rang the bell to Margaret's apartment. He hadn't seen Margaret since he was three, when she had returned home for Priscilla's funeral, but he was sure she'd be happy to see him. After all, she'd stood up for him when his mother said he was too young to have coffee, didn't she? She obviously had a soft spot for him. But when the door finally opened in response to the bell, the short dark-skinned woman who looked at him acted as if she were confronting a stranger.

"Yes?" the woman asked after giving him a thorough visual once-over.

"Excuse me, Ma'am. I'm looking for my sister, Margaret."

The woman paused, and then said, "There's no one here by that name."

Bumpy said he then looked at the address he'd copied and then said, "Are you sure?"

"Of course, I'm sure," the woman snapped. "And what do you want with her anyway?"

"Well, Ma'am, like I said, she's my sister. I haven't seen her in a long time. Not since she last visited the family back in Charleston some years back, but I thought I'd look her up now that I'm in New York," Bumpy explained. "I don't mean no harm, but I thought she might like to see me, too. Do you know where she lives?"

"No, I don't." The woman started to close the door, but the look on Bumpy's face must have melted her heart just a little. "So, are you doing well now that you're in New York?"

"Yes, Ma'am," Bumpy answered truthfully.

"Are you going to school?"

"Yes, Ma'am," Bumpy lied.

The woman nodded. "Well, that's good. I hope you have a nice day." With that she closed the door, leaving Bumpy standing out in the hallway thoroughly confused. Bumpy told me that he replayed the scene over and over in his head during the long subway ride home to Harlem.

When he got back to the apartment he was confronted by an angry Mabel – it seemed the Board of

Education finally got around to sending her a notice in the mail that Bumpy hadn't ever showed up to attend school.

Bumpy stood silently while Mabel screamed and yelled, and said he'd never amount to anything and that she was ashamed he was her own flesh and blood. When she finished he pulled out the paper with Margaret's address and handed it to her.

"Where did you get that?" Mabel screamed, snatching it out of his hand.

"Mabel, is that the right address for Margaret?" Bumpy asked quietly.

"I asked where'd you get it!"

"It doesn't matter. I just need to know if that's Margaret address."

It must have been the hurt in Bumpy's voice that calmed Mabel down, because then she put her hand on his shoulder and asked him what was wrong. Bumpy told her what happened that afternoon, then asked – again – if he'd copied the correct address. Mabel nodded, and asked him what the woman who answered the door looked like. When Bumpy described her, Mabel said sadly, "That was Margaret, Bumpy. I'm so sorry."

Bumpy turned around, but not before Mabel saw the tears that filled his eyes. She grabbed him in a hug and held him while he cried.

Afterward, Mabel wanted to call Margaret and tell her off, but Bumpy persuaded her not to, saying if she didn't want anything to do with him, that was fine, he didn't want anything to do with her. He never got over it, though. To the day he died he couldn't recount the story without his voice breaking.

Mabel still tried to insist that Bumpy start attending school, but she changed her tune when he showed her all the money he'd managed to put away during the months he'd been playing hooky. It was a total of two hundred dollars – a wondrous sum back in 1920. He told her that he'd made it sweeping sidewalks – conveniently leaving out the burglaries, the gambling, and the protection services – and said he wanted to send $100 home to their parents, and that she could have the rest of the money. Mabel readily agreed, and didn't say too much of anything again about him going to school.

By the 1920s Harlem was not just the largest black community in New York City, it was also the midnight playground for well-to-do whites looking for excitement.

They would arrive in their Jaguars, Studebakers, and Rolls Royces and chauffeured limousines to drink illegal booze at the nightclubs, most of which were owned by gangsters. People like the wild Gloria Vanderbilt (mother of the jeans empire mogul who bore her name), Jimmy Durante, Sid Graumann, Charlie Chaplin, Milton Berle, James Cagney, Fanny Brice, Bette Davis, Marlene Dietrich, were among the celebrities who frequented the exciting Cotton Club, opened by gangster Owney Madden (who was close friends with Bub Hewlett) in 1923. Duke Ellington was the first band leader of the club, followed by Cab Calloway, and frequent performers included the Nicolas Brothers, Louis Armstrong and Florence Mills.

The Harlem Renaissance was also in full swing. Writers like Langston Hughes, Countee Cullen, Claude McKay, Wallace Thurman, and Zora Neale Hurston were taking the literary world by storm.

There was a lot going on in Harlem. And of course there was more than enough going on to keep the Harlem Bad Men – whose number now included Bumpy and his crew -- busy and in the pink. Now they were no longer just providing protection for grocery store and restaurant owners, they were also offering their services to the owners of clubs and speakeasies. Not usually clubs like the Cotton Club and Connie's Inn, which catered only to white customers, but to the black establishments with mixed customers like The Hoofers, the Little Savoy, and the Sugar Cane.

It was Bub, who'd taken a liking to Bumpy, who suggested Bumpy and his crew also branch out and offer protection for numbers bankers in Harlem. These men, including Casper Holstein, Joe Ison, and Willie Brunder, were among the richest in Harlem, richer even than the night club owners – their number joints brought in thousands of tax-free dollars a week. The number bankers were serious about their protection, and wanted only the toughest and fiercest bodyguards in Harlem. Bumpy soon proved himself to be one of the best – so much so that he was soon one of the most sought after bodyguards in Harlem.

One evening in February 1924, while he and Nat were escorting a Cuban numbers banker named Alex Pompez home from a night partying in Spanish Harlem, a man came out from an alley brandishing a gun and demanded Pompez give him his wallet. In a flash, Bumpy drew his switchblade and cut a thin but deep slash across the man's cheek. The man dropped the gun, and Bumpy pushed Pompez back into the car, and then proceeded to slash the would-be thief's throat, and then slashed him across the abdomen for good measure.

A police officer on the corner heard the commotion and came running, but by then Bumpy had dropped his knife into the gutter and Nat kicked it into an open sewer. When the officer asked Bumpy what happened he said he didn't know, he'd only just arrived on the scene himself and found the man on the sidewalk trying to put his guts back in his stomach. The officer eyed him suspiciously, and then tried to question Pompez but Bumpy blocked his path, saying that the well-known numbers banker didn't speak English. The officer demanded that he move, but Bumpy refused, and told Nat to get in the drivers seat and get Pompez out of there. When the officer again tried to approach Pompez, Bumpy again blocked his path and this time the officer tried to push him out the way. Bumpy responded by punching him in the jaw, and the two began to fight, each only using only one hand -- the whole time Bumpy's left hand covered the officer's right to stop him from drawing his gun. It was only after three other officers arrived on the scene that they managed to subdue Bumpy, but by then Nat and Pompez were long gone.

The seventeen-year-old Bumpy was arrested and charged with assaulting an officer, resisting arrest, and attempted murder (the would-be thief actually survived the switchblade assault!). But by the time the lawyer the grateful Pompez obtained for him got through with the court system, Bumpy was only convicted for disorderly conduct and sentenced to a mere one-year probation. Pompez had good reason to be grateful – he'd made millions in the numbers racket but was trying to funnel his money into legitimate business enterprises. Always a baseball fanatic, Pompez, had just bought the Cuban Eastern Stars of the Eastern Colored League and the "New York Cubans" of the Negro League, and was in the process of helping to organize the first Negro League World Series in 1924 – he didn't need or want the bad press the knifing would be sure to generate. Later in life Pompez became the international scouting director for the New York Giants/San Francisco Giants. He was elected to the Baseball Hall of Fame in 2006.

When word spread of Bumpy's street heroics his reputation grew even further, and he was soon as much in demand as Bub. The one person not impressed with his new found fame, however, was Mabel. She was appalled when Bumpy's name appeared in the papers, and said she would never forgive him for shaming the Johnson name. She still accepted the money he gave her every week, though.

It was a couple of months later, on May 24th, that a killing occurred which shocked Harlem. Finley was holding one of his crap games in a basement at 129 West 134th Street, and after a couple hours of play a pimp known as Yellow Charleston went broke. Charleston tried to beg some money from Finley to get back in the game, but Finley refused – echoing the sentiment he had said so many years before, "I don't gamble against my own money." Charleston then turned to another player, John Parker, for a loan, but Parker agreed with Finley, adding that anyone who ran out of their own money needed to take the lesson learned and stay out the game. Yellow Charleston was furious, saying that he'd lost eight hundred dollars, and he wanted a chance to make his money back. Finley just waved his hand and said, "Nigga, get out the way so I can roll the dice." In response, Charleston pulled out a gun and shot Parker in the stomach. He then placed the gun against Finley's head and pulled the trigger, but the gun didn't go off. Charleston then ran from the basement and fled up the street to Seventh Avenue. He found Barron Wilkins standing outside his cabaret, The Exclusive Club, talking to a friend.

"Barron," Charleston said out of breath. "I need some money, man. I just shot a guy and I need $100 for a getaway."

Wilkins – who was 63 – was one of the most popular men in town, and was respected by all of the sporting men around in Harlem as a standup guy who would help a fellow out in a time of need. He'd been in the club business for more than 40 years, having opened his first club in the Tenderloin when that neighborhood was still populated with blacks. He was also the financier of Jack Johnson, the first black to win the boxing heavyweight championship, and was known as a philanthropist who financed all of the black baseball teams in New York. But while he knew Yellow Charleston, he didn't know him well. He looked at the man and said simply, "I ain't got that much money, man."

"You're right in front of your club!" Yellow Charleston said frantically. "You can just go in and get it. I need it, man. I need it bad."

Wilkins shook his head, and turned back to his friend. That's when Yellow Charleston pulled his gun out again and fired three shots into Wilkins' chest and stomach. He then stepped up and placed his gun against Wilkins' friend's face, but once again the gun failed to fire, and Yellow Charleston ran down Seventh Avenue.

A crowd quickly formed, and someone carried Parker up from the basement and placed him and Wilkins in a taxi and rushed off to Harlem Hospital, which was only a block away. Unfortunately, both died enroute.

Now, as you know, Finley was one of Bumpy's best friends; and Wilkins was one of Bub's. When the two of them heard what happened they combined forces and went looking for Yellow Charleston. Bumpy later told me that he wanted to get at Yellow Charleston because he tried to kill Finley, but Bub's grievance was the greater; he'd actually lost his good friend. They got to him before the police, and the man was never heard of again. When either was asked who did what to Yellow Charleston neither would answer directly, saying only that between them they got the job done – they avenged their friends. That's the kind of guys they were.

A few weeks later Bumpy started working for Madame Stephanie St. Clair. Like most people who heard about what he'd done for Pompez, she was impressed, and hired him to protect one of her many spots around Harlem. One day she saw him reading one of his favorite books, The Black Phalanx, which was a history of Negro soldiers in the United States. When she questioned him about the book he offered to let her borrow it saying he'd already read it about ten times, the first time when he was in elementary school. Impressed by his intelligence, she made him a personal bodyguard, and soon she had him escorting her to concerts and plays. Madame Queen was a cultured sort, and she and Bumpy liked to discuss the classics. But cultured or not, Queenie was also a wildcat, who would fight to protect what she called her own. Bumpy admired that about her as much as he admired her class. The two soon became fast friends.

But a year later Bumpy was sent to Elmira for ten years on a burglary charge, and did two years before making parole. Then in 1927 he was sentenced to another two years in Elmira on an assault charge. After doing his time for that he was back out on the streets for less than five months before being sent back up to Sing Sing on a grand larceny charge and sentenced to 2 years and six months. It was while he was there that he met Harold Guiliani – father of Rudy Guiliani, the former mayor of New York and Republican presidential candidate – who was doing time for assault.

But it was when he got out of prison for that hitch that the legend of Bumpy Johnson really began.

Chapter Four - The Tiger from Marseilles

According to my husband, anyone who knew Stephanie St. Clair knew she was not going to just roll over for anybody.

That's Madame Stephanie St. Clair if you please, or Madame Queen as her friends called her. Or as her enemies called her...the Tiger from Marseilles.

By 1932 Madame Queen had headed her medium-sized numbers operation for 10 years, and threats or no threats she was not going to obediently turn the reigns over to some Bronx bully, even if that bully was the notoriously bloodthirsty Dutch Schultz. "Ze God-damned Dutchman can keees my ass," she hissed. "He zinks I'm some stupid nigga? I show him he zinks wrong!"

Records show the Queen was born in Martinique, a small island in the East Caribbean, but had come to Harlem in 1912. The haughty and sophisticated Madame, however, told people that she was born in Marseilles, in "European France," and spoke flawless French, not patois, the pidgin french spoken by many in the Caribbean. "Moi? Je suis francaise," she would say when people questioned her nationality. She could also speak Spanish, and when she went off on one of her famous tirades, the Madame spat curses in all three languages. Although she at times had the mouth of a sailor, Madame Queen prided herself on always being dressed like a lady. She was usually tastefully attired in silk dresses – silvery-gray was her favorite color – often topped off with a snazzy hat cocked to the side, or sometimes a stylish turban. Perfect attire to wear to the operas she frequently attended, but also quite suitable for the jazz and honky-tonk music played at the Harlem speak-easies that the Queen also frequented.

The statuesque beauty never spoke about how she had raised the capital to start her numbers operation back in 1922, but her detractors snidely reminded people that her title was, after all, Madame. They never made such derogatory statements in front of her, though, because the 5-foot 8-inch, athletically built brown-skinned hellfire was quick to kick off her expensive high-heels and go toe-to-toe with any man or woman insolent enough to insult her breeding and character. It did not matter how Madame Queen had gotten into the number business -- what mattered was that she was not leaving without a fight.

The numbers game of Depression-era Harlem was the poor man's lottery. If a struggling family put down a dollar and picked the right three numbers they could get up to $600. In the 1920's most Harlemites were only making $10 or $15 a week, so a solid hit represented more than most of them earned in a year.

Not everyone could afford to play a dollar a day on a number, but most found a way to throw down something. A quarter could bring a lucky player $150, enough to buy a room full of furniture at Blumsteins on 125th Street, which didn't employ African-Americans but did sell to them. A dime could bring in $60, enough to pay the rent for a 3-bedroom apartment on St. Nicholas Avenue. A nickel investment could bring a return of $30, enough to buy back-to-school clothes at the open-air Market at 116th Street and Park Avenue. Even a single penny would bring in $6 -- enough for a weeks worth of ham hocks, greens and black-eyed peas. It's no wonder that most people in Harlem plunked down their hard-earned coins in hope of hitting the daily number.

And those hard-earned coins added up to quite a large amount of green dollars. According to testimony given during the Seabury investigations held in New York City in 1931, the numbers rackets in Harlem were raking in more than $50 million. An astounding figure, considering the fact that the country was in the midst of the Great Depression.

The number business was four-layered -- the number players, the number runners, the number controllers and the number bankers. The players were, of course, the people who handed over their money in hopes of beating the 1000-1 odds to get their 600-1 payoff. The number runners were the people who would go around everyday writing the player's number picks on individual slips of papers and collecting their money. Most number runners were on salary, but tradition held that when a person successfully hit on a number they would give the runner 10 percent.

Each day the number runner would turn the money and slips he had collected into the number controller, a kind of accountant or administrator, who tallied up the money and slips from the various runners (some operations had as many as 100 different runners) and kept track of how many people actually hit the number. The controller got 35 percent of the take for his trouble.

The controller would then turn over the daily receipts into the banker, who used his 65 percent of the take to pay off all hits and pay the ice -- the illegal payoffs to the police department, magistrates and judges -- so that their operations would not be busted.

Ice could run into tens of thousands of dollars a year; but even so, the bankers were happily rolling in dough. Wilfred Brunder, who originally hailed from Bermuda, was a shirt-maker before he started banking numbers in 1923. On the first day of his operation his take was a paltry $7.13, but by 1930 he was pulling in $11,000 a day. His annual income from his numbers operations was estimated to be more than $600,000 in 1930. Herbert Hoover, the U. S. president at the time, was earning a yearly salary of $75,000.

Enrique "Henry" Miro, a South American whom most Harlemites thought was Puerto Rican, was estimated to be making about $142,000 a year from his numbers operation.

The oddly named Casper Holstein, the great Harlem Renaissance benefactor, was known as the largest of the Harlem bankers. The Virgin Islands native was estimated to be bringing in close to $1 million a year from his operation.

Madame Queen was not one of the big-leaguers, her operation only brought in about $100,000 a year. But it was enough to keep her in silk gowns, as well as enough for her to purchase and fabulously furnish a number of expensive brownstones and maintain a stable of fine cars as well as a flat in the ritzy Colonial Parkway Apartments on Edgecomb Avenue. It was also enough to earn her the distinction of being the largest female banker in Harlem.

But "ze Goddamned Dutch Schultz" threatened to end all of that. Somehow the Dutch had become aware of the cash that was flowing around Harlem and he wanted a share.

Shortly after midnight on Saturday, September 22,1928, numbers king Casper Holstein, one of only six Negro millionaires in Harlem, was kidnapped by four white men as he got out of his chauffeured limousine to visit a married woman in the block of 145th Street and Seventh Avenue. The men at first told him they were cops, but once inside the car Holstein was beaten with a blackjack, bound and gagged. Holstein's chauffeur tried to follow the car but lost it in traffic. He then drove to the nearest police station to report the kidnapping.

The next afternoon employees at the Turk Club, a social club owned and operated by Holstein, received a call from the kidnappers demanding $17,000 for Holstein's release. Apparently surprised that no one tried to negotiate the ransom amount down, the kidnappers called back and upped the ante to $50,000. A third call was placed to the Turk Club, and this time the kidnappers put Holstein on the telephone. After assuring Turk Club manager Denis Armstead that he was okay, Holstein said, "Tell the police to get off the case or all they'll get is my dead body."

The ransom was paid, and Holstein was released shortly after midnight the following night. He told police that he did not know his abductors, and denied that a ransom had been paid. *The New York Times*, tipped off by police, reported the story. It is commonly believed that one of the kidnappers was Vincent "Mad Dog" Coll, who was later a bitter enemy of Dutch Schultz, but at the time was in the Dutchman's employ. Schultz now had proof that the numbers were not just a penny-ante racket. If Negroes could get their hands on $50,000 on a weekend – when financial institutions were closed – than that meant there was plenty more cash where that came from.

Dutch started sending his men to Harlem to tell the Negro numbers bankers that he was interested in joining their operation. In return, he told them, he would provide protection so that their operators would not be kidnapped, and also make sure that their operations would be left alone by the cops. Numbers bankers, however, already had their own protectors and they doubled up their bodyguards after the lightly-veiled threat by Schultz. Still, police officers who were already getting a healthy cut from the Negro bankers started making some arrests on Schultz's behalf.

Madame Queen began writing letters to the Negro newspapers, to the police commissioner and even the Mayor protesting that since Negro bankers were paying their ice they should not be getting arrested -- to do so she felt was a blatant show of discrimination against Negroes, and just plain dishonest. Then, in December 1929, Madame Queen was arrested as she stood in the hallway of an apartment building at 117 W. 141st Street, and sentenced to a year at Welfare's Island for racketeering. After a month in jail the Queen agreed to testify in the investigation being conducted by New York City Judge Samuel Seabury. It's believed that Seabury started his inquiry after white New Yorkers started questioning how Holstein, a Negro, could have amassed a fortune large enough for him to pay a $50,000 ransom.

Madame Queen gave the names of police officers and magistrates on the take, but only those who had crossed her and other Negroes -- the ones who took their money but continued to arrest and levy jail sentences against them. The Seabury investigators also subpoenaed other Negro bankers to testify, but feeling it would be more in their interest to disappear than to appear before the tribunal, many fled.

Brunder and Miro were two of the number bankers who decided to take a puff and fled the country in early 1931. Both turned their number operations, although not their assets, over to Joseph Matthias Ison, a former elevator operator who had been a faithful collector for both men. But shortly after his windfall Big Joe, as he was called, was visited by two white men demanding a substantial cut of his new business, and threatening to take it over his dead body if he didn't willingly turn it over.

71

Ison could have gone to one of the well-known Harlem protectors, like big bad William "Bub" Hewlett, or his side-kick Malcolm "Blue" Renier, for help; but Ison didn't want the likes of them sniffing around his new business, so instead he turned to Bronx attorney J. Richard "Dixie" Davis for advice.

Davis told Ison he'd be glad to help him, and that he had a client named Arthur Fleggenheimer, also known as Dutch Schultz, who would be more than glad to provide the protection from the bullies. Coincidentally, Davis told Ison, Schultz was looking to get into the numbers operation himself. What Davis failed to say was that it was two of Dutch Schultz's men, Abe "Bo" Weinberg and Abe Landau, who had threatened Ison in the first place. A meeting was set-up between Ison and George Weinberg, Bo's older brother, and a price of $600 weekly was agreed upon for Schultz's protection. That was about triple the amount Ison would have paid someone like Hewlett, but he knew that after going to Schultz turning down his offer could be bad for his health.

In May of 1931, Henry Miro came back on the scene and told Ison he wanted his bank back. But Ison by now had grown accustomed to the thousand dollars a week he was making off of the operation. He told Miro that he had to talk to Schultz about stepping back in, and Miro reluctantly agreed. The meeting was set-up by Davis at the swanky east 98th Street apartment of his girlfriend. Ison told Schultz and Davis that he didn't think Miro should be able to just come back and claim his bank after all the hard work he had put into maintaining it. Caught off-guard, Miro's hot Latin temper flared and he began cursing at Ison, furious that his once faithful employee had set him up. Miro jumped up from his chair and tried to get at Ison, but was pulled back by Schultz's bodyguards. Then Schultz calmly asked the furious Miro to step into the kitchen for a moment. There Schultz, who was flanked by two gunmen, said to Miro, "Henry, do what I say or I will kill you." Miro had known Schultz for years -- he had often bought Schultz's bootleg liquor for the couple of speak-easies that he owned – and hot-tempered though Miro might be, he knew that Schultz was quite capable of carrying out that dastardly threat right there on the spot. It was a well-known fact that Schultz had one time shot and killed a man -- his business partner, Jules Martin-- in a hotel room when negotiations weren't going in the Dutchman's favor. After a moment, Miro simply smiled and said, "Why, Arthur, you know I always do what you say."

By the time the angry but restrained Miro left the apartment Ison owned 1/3rd of his bank, and Schultz's gang had been "hired" to protect the other 2/3rds.

Then, on Black Wednesday, the day before Thanksgiving, a heavily played number 527 came out, and Harlem bankers were scrambling to pay off all of their hits. Big Joe had to wipe out his entire bank in order to pay off all his customers, and was still $18,000 shy. It wasn't unusual for other number bankers to bail out a colleague in such situations, but they all had been hit hard. Big Joe turned to someone he knew had money to loan -- Dutch Schultz.

Dixie arranged another meeting at his girl friend's apartment, and when Ison arrived he found both George and Bo Weinberg sitting in the living room. A few minutes later Schultz arrived, unbuttoned the jacket of his cheap suit, pulled out the loaded .45 he kept tucked in his pants and placed it on the table in front of him. The negotiations then began.

Schultz agreed to furnish the loan, but in return he wanted a 2/3rds cut of Ison's business. Ison's 1/3rd was to come out of the profits from the operation, and in addition Ison was to get a $200 weekly salary from the bank. It was a ridiculous offer, but one that Ison didn't see how he could refuse, considering that cold black loaded pistol on the table.

As it worked out, Ison never saw his 1/3 share of the take. Although by Ison's count the bank was taking in about $7,000 a day Schultz said every cent of it was going towards paying expenses. Dutch Schultz now had a firm foothold in the Harlem number business and he continued to expand his number empire, which he called his "Combination."

Late in 1931 Madame Queen was visited by Bub Hewlett, now working for Schultz. He told her that it would be in her best interests to join the Combination, which now included the operations of most of the big-time Negro bankers. But Madame had already heard how Miro, Ison and even her friend Brunder -- who had also come back to reclaim his operation -- had gone from netting tens of thousands of dollars a week to receiving only a $100-200 salary. Madame flew into a rage at Hewlett's friendly suggestion. She would never, never, never, surrender her operations to "Ze Goddamned Dutchman," she told him. And how dare he, a Negro, even approach her with such a ludicrous offer on behalf of a white man.

Bub tried to calm her, and suggested that she should at least meet with Schultz before making up her mind. It was then that the furious Queen told Bub, a 6-1 footer built like a line-backer, that not only could "Ze Dutchman keees my ass," but Bub could help him do it. Not many people could talk to Bub in such a manner and continue to enjoy good health. Harlem legends are still told about the many men that Bub had sent to Harlem Hospital for much less -- but those were men, and Queen was well . . . a lady. Albeit one with a mouth like a gutter. The only thing Bub bestowed on Madame Queen that day was a snarl, and a departing sarcastic comment that she might not find her next callers as gentlemanly as he.

Within just a few days Madame Queen began to feel the heat. Her number spots, where the number runners would drop off their slips and money to the controllers -- were all of a sudden the target of drive-by shootings. Her employees were savagely beaten, and threatened that if they continued to work for the Queen they would receive much worse. Police officers to whom she had continued to faithfully pay ice were all of sudden busting her people, a serious problem for any numbers banker. If a number runner was busted before he dropped off his work to the controller, or if the controller was busted before his work had been shipped to the bank, not only would the money that was on them at the time be confiscated, but also the numbers slips which showed what numbers customers had played. The word quickly spreads in the street when customers don't get paid when they hit a number, and business begins to drop off as customers start doing business with number operations that would pay off.

Madame began to complain to police brass that as long as she paid her ice she should be left alone. In December of 1931 she threatened to sue the *Inter-State Tattler*, a colored newspaper based in Harlem, when that paper published articles that she was trying to frame colored policemen. She wasn't trying to frame anyone, she said, she just wanted to get the protection for which she was paying. She was also furious because the paper also intimated that she was involved in a sexual relationship with her female secretary.

But despite all of her troubles, the Madame managed to maintain her numbers operation, although on a smaller scale. Surprisingly many of her employees stuck with her despite the frequent episodes of violence. She had a way of motivating them, with money and with the challenge "I will stand up to ze Goddamned Dutchman and I am a lady. You are men, and you will desert me now? What kind of men would desert a lady in a fight?" She encouraged other Negro numbers bankers to remain independent from Schultz's Combination. "You cannot let some goddamned white man come and take over ze colored operations. What kind of men are you?" Some did try to resist the Jewish gangster, but eventually buckled under the heavy-pressure tactics carried out by Schultz's white hoodlums and the Hewlett gang.

Alexander Pompez, the well-known and well-liked "El Cubano," was one of the bankers who tried to hold out, but after numerous visits by Schultz thugs, and two "escorted visits" to see the Dutchman he too finally capitulated. But still the Queen held on -- even though Schultz's men were now shooting up her spots on a regular basis and putting the word out that since she would not cooperate they were planning to "put her on the spot." In other words, to kill her. One time the elegant Madame Queen had to hide in a coal bin in the basement of one of her spots to escape Schultz's thugs.

Then, in July 1932, one of Schultz's men, Max Renney, approached Catherine Odlum, an attorney and a good friend of Madame Queen. He offered Odlum $500 to lure the Queen to Odlum's apartment so that he could kill her. When Odlum refused he revised his request, and promised that if Odlum could get the Queen to come to Odlum's apartment building he would do the stabbing in the hallway rather than in the apartment. Odlum pretended consent, but quickly ran back to the Queen to inform her of the plot.

The two women then went to the Detectives Division of the 32nd precinct to swear out a complaint against Renney and Schultz, but the sergeant there said he could not do anything. The Queen accused him of being one of the men on the Dutch's payroll and reminded him that she also paid ice. The sergeant told her there was nothing he could do, but if she wanted to she could go to the Washington Heights Magistrate's Court to possibly get the warrants. Not too many known number bankers would be willing to go into court for any reason, but not too many known number bankers were like the Queen. On September 15, the Queen and Odlum appeared before Judge Louis Brodsky seeking an arrest warrant for Max Renney.

But Brodsky, after listening to the two women, expressed disbelief in the seriousness of the affair. The Queen, in true character, flew into a rage. "Zat's why zhere is so much crime in zees United States," she screamed. Then, with a disdainful gesture and head held high, she walked away from the Bench and towards the courtroom exit.

"Come back here, you," called the judge. "Don't you walk out on me . . . and never mind all this crime in the United States." The bailiff rushed over to the Queen who was forced to reapproach the Bench. After a dressing down from Brodsky, the Queen told the judge that if he were afraid to send the police make the arrest she herself would be willing to go into "Renney's bedroom" to do the deed herself if Brodsky would only give her the proper documentation to do so. The exasperated judge denied the application.

That same day the two women appeared before Chief Magistrate James E. MacDonald to apply for a bench warrant for the arrest of Schultz himself. "Dutch's men know I am ze only one in Harlem who can take back from zere boss the racket he stole from my colored friends," she told the astonished judge. "And zey know I'm getting ready to go into action.

That's why zey want me knifed." But MacDonald also turned her down.

Undaunted, the Queen went to City Hall the following day and demanded to see Mayor Joseph V. McKee. When told he was unavailable she brushed past the clerks and secretaries and headed straight for the Mayor's private office. She was intercepted by McKee's police aide, Lt. James Harten who told the woman that the Mayor was in the midst of a conference of more pressing matters, but that he, Harten, would see to it that the Harlem police would protect her.

A few days after her unsatisfying trip to City Hall, Madame Queen had her chauffeur drive her to the offices of *The Amsterdam News* to complain to reporters about the treatment she was receiving from legal authorities. Finding the journalists only mildly interested in her story, she then went to 125th Street and Seventh Avenue. It was one of the corners where people normally gathered to while away hours listening to the soap-box preachers and wait for the daily number to come out. She climbed out of her expensive limousine and started berating the people for doing business with number bankers under Dutch Schultz's control. "Hees stores are taking $10,000 a day out of Harlem," she told them. "Zey pay hits, yes. But zen zey send out men to hold you up a block away and take away ze money. I know what I'm talking about."

She promised that the white racketeer was going to get put out of Harlem, even if she had to personally put a picket at every one of his number spots from 125th to 155th streets. "Who does he zink he ees?" she hissed. Then snapped her fingers and answered her own question. "He's Nobody! I'm going to show him something and he better get out of Harlem before I begin."

There were some people out there who thought the Queen was crazy, after all she had gone to the police, she had gone to the courts, and she had gone to City Hall, and it was evident that she would be getting no support from any of those quarters. And feisty and admired as Madame Queen was in Harlem, she was still just one woman. But Madame Stephanie St. Clair had a secret weapon. She knew what she was saying when she said she was getting ready to go into action, even if nobody else knew. Since July she had been in touch with one person that she knew was always ready for a fight, and resented as much as she did white people trying to take something from Negroes. She knew that in the following month, in October, that person was coming back to Harlem. She knew that after 2 1/2 years in prison, Bumpy Johnson was getting out of Sing Sing. And she knew that the Dutchman was in trouble.

Chapter Five – A War in Harlem

"I see you made it home," Bub said slapping Bumpy over his shoulder. "Welcome back. How'd they treat you up there?"

"How you think?" Bumpy answered.

"Like shit."

"Well," Bumpy said with a smile. "You got it right."

The two friends laughed, and Bub slapped him on the back again and ordered two ginger ales, which the bartender hurried and put before them. He knew, as many did, what the two Harlem Bad Men were getting ready to discuss and, like the many, he didn't know how it was going to turn out. Everyone knew that Bub was already working for Dutch Schultz, and it was common knowledge that he was going to want Bumpy working for him – or at least with him. Trouble was everyone knew that Madame Queen was hoping that Bumpy would take her side in the battle. What no one knew was which side Bumpy, who had just turned 25, was going to take.

That bartender is still alive, and he expressly requested that I not mention his name or the bar he worked in because he doesn't want anyone asking him questions about the episode this late in life. I don't know why, since he told everyone else in Harlem about the discussion shortly after it occurred. And it isn't like Bumpy didn't tell me about the conversation later, but I made the promise and I'll keep it.

So anyway, Bub tells Bumpy that he's got work for him.

"Yeah? What?" Bumpy asked.

"Same thing you was doing before you left the streets. Just keeping folks in line, making sure they do what they supposed to do and making sure they don't do what they ain't supposed to do," Bub answered.

"And what they ain't supposed to be doing is writing numbers for anyone but that Jew guy, Shultz, huh?"

Bub looked at him in surprise. "So you heard, huh?"

Bumpy nodded. "Yeah, I heard while I was in the joint. They say the Jew guy been taking over the numbers in Harlem. Said he's hired a bunch of treacherous coloreds to beat up on other coloreds. You heard anything about that?"

At this point, the bartender told me, he pulled out a rag and started wiping down the bar, ready to duck down cause he just knew there was gonna be some shooting up in there. But Bub just looked at Bumpy and said, "You grown now, little nigger? Cause it seems like you're smelling yourself."

"Do it?"

"You so grown you think you gonna try me?"

Bumpy shook his head. "Nah, I ain't trying to try you. But I'm not expecting you to try me, either. I ain't in the shit, and I don't see any reason to get in it."

Bub smiled. "Good to hear."

"At least not right now."

"What's that supposed to mean?"

"It means I only been out two days, so I gotta get the lay of the land again.See what I'm gonna be doing," Bumpy responded.

"You work for Dutch and I can guarantee you $200 a week," Bub said.

"I heard you getting paid three hundred."

Bub laughed. "Oh, so now you think you should be getting what I get? I told you that you smelling yourself. But youse a good man. Let me talk to Schultz and see what he says. I'm sure we can work something out."

Bumpy shook his head. "Naw, don't do that. I can't ever see myself siding with the white man over the black man. You do what you gotta do, and I'll see what I'ma be doing."

"Fair enough," Bub said. "But I expect I'll hear from you what you gonna be doing before I hear from anyone else."

"Solid."

Bub extended his hand. "Gimme some skin."

The two men touched hands, and the bartender finally exhaled.

***

"I don't need you to protect me. I can protect myself," Madame Queen shouted at Bumpy later that night. "I want to take care of ze damn Dutchman. Run heem out of Harlem and back to ze damn Bronx where he belongs. Or better yet keel heem, and put heem out hess misery."

"But Queenie –"

"No! No, but Queenie! I want you to keel heem or I keel heem myself. You gonna be like ze rest of zeese scaredy men? You? Hah! I speet on the whole lot of you."

Bumpy sighed and shook his head. "Queenie, you know I'm not scared. But what you're talking about is an all out war."

"Boy, when I first seen you, you was reading a book about colored men and war. Now I give you ze chance to be one."

"Yeah, well they had the whole United States government financing those wars. Who's going to finance yours?"

"You tink me got no money? I got plenty money."

"Well, it's going to take a lot more than just plenty of money," Bumpy said. "Figure you're gonna have to pay at least two hundred a week each for good men, and even if you only have ten – which really ain't near enough – that's two thousand a week. And in addition to the men you gotta buy guns, and pay off the cops, and put up bails. And this is not going to be a matter of days or weeks. This is going to take months. Maybe years. Hell, you think you've got enough money to last that long? Especially with your spots being hit every other day?"

"Well, we make zese other bankers pay. Zat's what we do. We all cheep in and zhen you get your guns and your men. And zen you keel ze Dutchman."

So Queenie and Bumpy called a meeting, and dozens of the colored bankers, comptrollers, and number runners showed up. But do you know not but more than a handful said they wanted to get involved? Most said they didn't think that Bumpy could win the war and they would just be losing their money and maybe their lives if Dutch Schultz found out they were working against him. But there were a few who stood up and said they'd back Bumpy. Alex Pompez was one – the Cuban who Bumpy used to work for before he got sent up to Sing Sing. Said he wouldn't do any fighting, but he'd donate money to the cause. He was already under the Schultz's thumb, but he resented it and wanted to be his own man again. Johnny Walker, who had a numbers bank in Sugar Hill, was also under Dutch's thumb. He didn't even attend the meeting, but contacted Bumpy later and told him that he couldn't donate a lot, but he'd do what he could. As long as Bumpy made sure Schultz didn't find out that he was aiding and abetting the enemy.

And there were people outside the numbers game who were willing to throw in with Bumpy, if not their body at least their wallet. One was Eddie Smalls.

Edwin Smalls was born in Charleston, like Bumpy, but in 1882. He moved to New York in 1909 and got a job as an elevator man in Harlem, and after saving a little money he opened a tiny pool joint on Fifth Avenue near 141st Street. But then Prohibition hit, and Eddie Smalls turned that pool joint into a gin joint with the quickness. Soon he tossed the junk out of the basement and expanded, bringing in live entertainment and naming the place Smalls Cafeteria. Most of his clientele were black, though there was a few whites who'd stop in, but by 1925 Eddie had made enough money to open a bigger and much grander club on the corner of 135th Street and Seventh Avenue. You might have heard of the place – Smalls Paradise.

Man, Smalls Paradise was grand! It could hold 1,500 customers and was right up there with the Cotton Club and Connie's Inn as the most well-known spots in Harlem. But unlike those two white-owned clubs, black as well as white were welcome to come spend their money at Smalls, buying bootleg liquor and being entertained by Charleston dancing waiters. Smalls made more money on Prohibition than any other black man in New York, and he knew how to spread his money around in all the right places. Like the white club owners, he paid off the cops on a regular basis so he wouldn't get busted, but he also made sure to find out the police captain's birthdays and such and sent them birthday cards stuffed with money. He did the same for the local politicians. Eddie Smalls could afford to be generous, his place was estimated to be raking in $10,000 a week – and that's without counting the money taken in on illegal booze and not reported to the

IRS. There was no doubt that by 1932 Smalls was already a millionaire.

Eddie Smalls had been one of the first of the black club owners to hire Bumpy, not that he needed protection – no one bothered Smalls' place – but because he wanted to give his fellow Charlestonite a break.

Eddie Smalls didn't hate white people, but he didn't love them either – although they made up a large part of his patronage. He got along with everyone but, like Bumpy, he preferred doing business with a black man over a white any day. He bristled about Dutch Schultz's takeover of the numbers racket, but it was none of his affair. But when he heard that Madame Queen and Bumpy were trying to raise money he didn't wait for them to come to him – he sought them out.

Madame Queen did approach Dickie Wells, though.

It's amazing to me that no one ever talks about Dickie Wells anymore, because back in the 1920s, 30s, and 40's, he was one of the most well known people in the entire city. Yes, the entire city. Not just Harlem, but the entire city. In fact, he was called "Mr. New York."

He was an amazing man, Mr. Dickie Wells. There's never been anyone like him. He was born in Harlem, in 1905, the youngest son of Carrie Wells, a coal black illiterate washwoman. I don't know who his father was, and chances are he didn't know either. He had an older brother and sister, both as dark as his mother, but Dickie was copper-skinned with dark wavy hair, and amazing good looks. Rumor was his daddy was white. Maybe so, but Dickie never claimed to be anything but black, which was very unusual back then since most black people who could get away with it claimed to be part white, or part Indian, or part Spanish . . . anything but all black. Remember, this was way before the time of black pride. That didn't come around until decades later.

Dickie was a change-of-life baby, both his siblings were in their teens by the time he was born, and his mother doted on him. She didn't have much money, but what she had she didn't mind spending on him. He was smart, but I don't know that he ever went far in school, but he did get a Ph.D from U.C.L.A., aka the University of the Corner of Lenox Avenue. Dickie took to the streets early, learning how to gamble, play the con, but most importantly, he learned how to dance. No, he didn't go to any dance school, but back then most black dancers didn't, they learned by hanging around the club dancers, studying their steps, and then going out on the corner and doing those steps over and over again until they mastered them. Dickie became so good that by the time he was in his teens he and two friends formed a group called Wells, Mordecai & Taylor.

They started out in the gin joints and speakeasies in Harlem, like Smalls Cafeteria and Mom's Club on 121st and Lenox, but they were so good they eventually moved to bigger spots like the Cotton Club and, of course, later to Smalls Paradise.

All of those boys could dance, but Dickie was the star, which was why his name was first on the billing. Not just because he was the best dancer – and he was – but he had this way of fixing his gaze on a woman while he danced, and almost hypnotize her. Dickie was handsome, and not in that almost effeminate way of Rudolph Valentino or one of those dandies, but a masculine handsome like Clark Gable. But more importantly he was blessed with what they now call bedroom eyes. When he smiled, his eyelids just naturally closed halfway over his eyes, giving it a soulful and sexy look, and women would just go wild.

It wasn't that Dickie did it on purpose, at least not at first, it was just how he smiled. Women would jam the clubs whenever the group was playing a joint, and the club owners soon realized it and the group got even more bookings. It was while dancing at the Cotton Club, I think when Dickie fully realized the power he had over women. It was in the 1920s, when blacks were allowed to work at the Cotton Club, but weren't allowed to patronize the club.

Dickie's group was on the floor doing their routine, and as usual Dickie fixed his gaze on a beautiful woman sitting at one of the tables near the dance floor. Since it was a white only club it was, of course, a white woman -- and one wearing an ermine stole, and with diamonds dripping from her ears, wrists, and fingers. Well, by the time the group's routine was half over the woman was near hyperventilating. But just at this time, the group went from tapping into a shimmy, and Dickie put his hands on his waist, did a slow sensuous turn, and started gyrating his hips, then fixed his gaze on another woman. Well, do you know that ermine stoled woman jumped up, stomped over to that other woman's table and threw a drink in her face? A cat fight ensued, and the club almost had to close down for the night. And keep in mind, Dickie had never met – or even seen – either woman before in his life!

Dickie was already making hundreds of dollars a week dancing – at a time when most black men were making only $25 or $35 a week – but that's when he realized he could be making a lot more money. If women were willing to fight over him just to be the beneficiary of one of his smiles, he was sure they would whip out their diamond studded purses and pay his company for a night of smiles. And he was so right. He was soon known as the Ebony Lorathio, and to this day I don't even know who Lorathio was, but he must have been a heckuva lover because Dickie certainly was – or so I heard. And the rumors had to be true, because Dickie became one of the wealthiest men in Harlem. He still danced with Wells, Mordecai & Taylor – and even toured the world with that troupe, but there was no doubt that he was more well-known as a gigolo than as a dancer.

Dickie was the most suave and sophisticated man I've ever met, black or white. He was charming. That's what he was. When he was introduced to a woman, instead of shaking her hand, he would simply hold it in his own – though just for a fleeting moment – as if it were the most fragile and precious thing in the world.

He had this way of making you feel that when he was with you no one else in the universe mattered. And he knew how to compliment a woman – on the color of her eyes, or the shape of her lips, or her intelligence. He always knew the right thing to say and exactly the right time to say it. But most importantly, when he looked at you he made you feel like he was looking at the most beautiful woman in the world.

Women loved him, and would vie for his attention with their pocketbooks. They gave him money, jewels, and cars. His conquests included socialites, famous singers, and even movie stars. Tallulah Bankhead (who was born in Alabama, that good old Confederate state) is said to have fainted when she heard he died. Ava Gardner (who was born in North Carolina) was said to have given him a cigarette holder made of solid gold, and engraved "from A to D" as well as a diamond encrusted watch, gold cuff links and a diamond tie pin to go with the silk ties she also bought for him. Even Joan Crawford, who wasn't exactly known for her fondness of blacks, invited Dickie to visit her whenever he was in California.

There were two things that made Dickie Wells really special – one was that men adored him just as much as women. No, not in that way – although I'm sure there were plenty of men who had their crushes on him – I'm talking about men kind of men. Like Clark Gable – the King of Hollywood – who once told Dickie that he had to bow down to the master when it came to women. Errol Flynn, Charlie Chaplin, and James Cagney were also among the male movie stars who always stopped by whatever club Dickie was appearing in when they were in New York. Even newspaper reporters liked Dickie. The only time this notorious gigolo ever got bad press was when the daughter of a Swedish diplomat had a nervous breakdown because Dickie was no longer paying attention to her and she revealed that she had abandoned her children to be with him.

But the thing that made Dickie really special, as far as I was concerned, was that he never ever took a dime from a black woman. He would siphon every dollar he could from the rich white women who were willing to pay for his affections, and then come uptown to Harlem and spend his money partying with the most beautiful black women of the day. Margherite Chapman (who later married Willie Mays), and Jean Parks (sister of Henry Parks, who founded Parks Sausages) were two of his favorite hang-out partners, but he was also a favorite of Madame Stephanie St. Clair. He also bought his mother, Carrie, a brownstone on 139th Street on Strivers Row – one of the most elite neighborhoods in Harlem. He moved into the basement apartment of the brownstone, and lived there until his death.

He also opened up the Hoofers Club on Seventh Avenue near 133rd Street where fledging tap dancers could come and practice their routines. The club never made any money, but Dickie didn't care – he ran the joint for the fun of it. The club was depicted in the movie Cotton Club, but they never mentioned Dickie Wells' name.

Many of his white female conquests would tell him that they didn't believe he was really all black, and that he looked like he could be Cuban. At that point he would invite them to visit his residence. The thing was he didn't tell them that he occupied the basement apartment, so when they walked up the stairs and rang the bell they would be face-to-face with coal-black and ever protective Carrie, who would look them up and down with disdain and ask them what they wanted with her son. Rumor has it that Ava Gardner broke a heel running back down those steps and into her waiting limousine.

It's a damn shame that people don't remember who Dickie Wells was, because he was a really good guy.

In 1932, when Stephanie St. Clair asked him to donate money to buy guns and supplies to support the coming numbers war with Dutch Schultz, he didn't blink an eye – he pledged a thousand dollars to the cause, even though he had nothing to do with the numbers racket. But when he found out that Bumpy was going to be the main combatant against Schultz, Dickie went back to Madame Queen and said he'd rethought his generous offer and had to withdraw it. When Madame Queen flew at him in a rage he caught her by the wrists and pulled her into an embrace.

"Calm down, Queenie," he crooned into her ear, "I'm actually changing my donation to make it an open checkbook." He then led her into a sensuous tango, and the two drank and partied it up for the rest of the night.

With Madame Queen, Pompez, Smalls, Wells, and a few others – like the big time dope dealer Wesley

Goodwin – willing to lay out the money, Bumpy next had to find the men who would act as soldiers. And of course, the men he turned to were his old friends.

"Shit, I ain't no fighter," Finley growled at the first meeting. "And I ain't taking no bullet for no one on a 'just because' tip."

"Nigger, ain't no one expecting *you* to fight. You're more useful in other ways," Bumpy said. "We're gonna need guns. And a lot. And stuff that can't be traced. You got a connect?"

"Stupid fucking question," Finley replied. "Let me know what you want and I'll get you the price. 'Course I'll be taking a little bit off the top for me."

"Okay, then," Bumpy said. He turned to Nat Pettigrew. "Nat –"

"Yeah, I'm in," Nat said before he could finish the question. "I ain't never shot a Jew before, but I guess they ain't no different from no one else. I want a .38, though. I can use .35's, but I prefer .38s."

"I'm in to," Junie said. "How much we getting paid?"

Bumpy laughed. "Two hundred."

"A month," Junie asked.

"A week."

"Hell, yeah, I'm in," Junie said rubbing his hands together.

Six-n-Eight, Obadiah, Ritchie Williams, Hoss Steele, Georgie Rose and Steve Mitchell also said they were down for the cause. Now Steve Mitchell knew he shouldn't have said nothing because he was a numbers controller himself – not for Dutch Schultz, but for the Italians. Oh yes, the Italians had their spots on the East Side of Harlem even then, but they let it be known to Dutch not to mess with any of their numbers guys. And they let their numbers guys know not to do anything to cross Schultz.

91

"How you going to be down for the cause when you down with the Italians?" Bumpy asked Steve Mitchell. "They find you involved they'll cut you loose and might even cut you up."

"Shit," Steve said, "you know I ain't letting you guys have all the fun. Besides, me and Nat are the only ones who even knows how to shoot straight. Don't worry. I'll just do my stuff on the sly. The guineas won't even have to find out. I'm not trying to lose the five hundred a week I'm getting from them at the numbers spot for the measly two hundred y'all getting."

The men walked out and headed down Seventh Avenue when Bumpy saw Bub Hewlett across the street standing on the corner in front of Smalls Paradise. "Y'all stay here, but stay in plain sight," he told his friends.

"Hey, Bub," he said when he walked over to the older man.

"Hey."

"I've been looking for you."

Bub looked at him suspiciously, and eased his hand to his pocket. "For what?"

Nat must have seen Bub's move toward his pocket because he called out, "Bumpy, you alright, man?"

Bumpy gave a wave in his direction, but kept his eye on Bub, whose hand remained in his pocket. "I told you I'd let you know what I was gonna be doing, remember?" Bumpy told him.

"And?"

"I'm working for Queenie."

"Man, you making the wrong move," Bub said. "The Queen's going down. The writing is on the wall."

"Yeah?" Bumpy gave a smile. "Well, you can call me and my men over there," he pointed to his crew, "a damn good set of erasers."

"Is that a fact?" Bub said with some amusement.

"It is," Bumpy answered.

"You know that means you're going up against me and my men."

"I know. The shit's gonna get interesting." Bumpy laughed.

Bub hesitated, then joined in with the laughter. He slowly eased his hand out of his pocket, and said, "Gimme some skin." The two men touched hands, then Bub said, "I guess I'll be seeing you around, Bumpy."

"Yeah, man. But I'm banking on seeing you first." With that the two burst out in laughter again, and then Bumpy walked back across the street and Bub disappeared into the club.

"I feel like the president of the United States," he told Junie as they resumed their march down Seventh Avenue.

"How's that?" Junie asked.

"I just declared war," Bumpy answered, "and you guys are my army. Now we gotta come up with a battle plan."

The first matter was getting guns, and Finley was the right choice for that job. In all the years I've known him Finley never paid the asking price for anything. He was the guy who would go into a fancy seafood restaurant, pull a waiter over and say, "Listen. I want the lobster, which goes for eight bucks. The shrimp goes for three. How about you write down that I ordered shrimp, you bring me the lobster, and I'll pay you the three for the check and slip another two in your pocket."

Nine times out of ten the waiter would go along with the plan, and in the case of the one time out of ten the waiter didn't, Finley would walk out and go to another restaurant with more understanding waiters.

Even when cable television came out in New York in the eighties, Finley figured out how to beat the system. He was living at the Lenox Terrace at the time, and he caught the cable guy going into someone's apartment for an installation and cut a deal for the guy to come to his flat and install cable for a one-time rate of fifty bucks. Finley had free cable until he died in 2002. But in addition to that, Finley wasn't a punk. When the going got tough Bumpy knew that he could count on Finley to pull out the little Derringer he carried in his breast pocket for emergencies and do some serious damage.

In Junie, Bumpy had a set of brains working for him that was as tight as a steel trap. While Bumpy was a planner, Junie was one of those people who could quickly take in a situation and make it work for him. I remember once Sarah Vaughn and her husband George Treadwell were at the Vets Club partying and some guy shot an acquaintance of Junie's named Jay-Jay. Well, after the shooting, Junie saw George slip a gun out of his pocket and handed it to Sarah who slipped it into her purse. Junie sidled up to Sarah and told her that he knew it was her husband who had shot Jay-Jay, and unless she ponied up five hundred dollars he was going to turn him in. Sarah protested that it wasn't George who shot Jay-Jay and for Junie to get out of her face. She then turned to Bumpy and said, "Bumpy, you know George didn't shoot Jay-Jay."

Junie looked Bumpy straight in the eye and said, "He shot him, man."

Bumpy shrugged and said, "If Junie said he shot him then I believe he shot him. And you know your man shouldn't go around shooting people. I suggest you pay up."

Sarah was pissed, and she gave Junie the $500 on the spot. As Junie and Bumpy were leaving the club he gave Bumpy half of the money.

"Did George really shoot Jay-Jay?" Bumpy asked as he slipped the money into his pocket.

"Naw, man. Paulie shot that nigger. I just saw a way to make a quick buck."

Bumpy shook his head and said, "You ain't shit, man."

Junie simply said, "Ain't that the truth."

As for Nat Pettigrew and Steve Mitchell, they were the two most cold-blooded men I've ever met. Stone-cold killers. There's some people who don't seem to know fear, and that's how Nat, and Steve were. They had no problems using guns, knives or their bare fists to take care of someone who needed taking care of. A couple of years ago I was watching a television program where they talked about some people whose brains are wired in such a way that they don't recognize fear the way most people do. I think that's how Nat and Steve were, and Bumpy, too. I've never known any of them to back down from a situation even when the guy they were facing had a gun and they didn't. Might be why they all got shot up so much.

Georgie Rose was a natural con man and smooth talker who was always able to find out who had information and figure out how to get it out of them. He was a dapper guy, who always wore a white carnation in his lapel, and the ladies loved him. Not only was he able to pass on the info he learned during the pillow talk of Dutch Schultz's men's girlfriends, he considered himself as much a fighter as a lover.

Obadiah wasn't as ruthless as the others, but he was brave and loyal.

Six-n-Eight, Hoss, and Ritchie Williams . . . well, they weren't as brave as the others, but they were the kind of the guys who would just go along to get along, and since their friends were in the battle then they were, too. Especially since they were going to get paid.

So it was the ten of them against the Dutch Schultz mob, but they figured they could handle it, and it turned out they could and they did.

Soon it wasn't just Madame Queen and the other bankers who had resisted joining the "Combination" who were getting their number spots shot up, it was Dutch Schultz spots, too. And it wasn't just the rogue bankers men who were being shot – the Dutchman's men were being shot and killed also.

Back then it was common courtesy that if you shot or beat someone into unconsciousness, you then hauled them into a car or a cab and then dumped them on the sidewalk in front of Harlem Hospital. In fact, the practice was so common that the hospital actually kept a gurney in the lobby to haul in the badly wounded men. This was a courtesy the Dutch Schultz men never gave, and so it was a courtesy they never received; prompting the African-American newspaper The New York Age to comment with awe – and perhaps some glee – about the number of white men found dead in Mount Morris Park during this time.

Bumpy and his crew of nine waged a guerilla war of sorts, and picking off Dutch Schultz's men was easy since there were few other white men walking around Harlem during the day. Bumpy and his men, however, blended in easily.

But Bub Hewlett and his men – which included Alfred Vincent, Fitzgerald "Fitzie" Grant, Malcolm "Blue" Renier, and William Pennyfeather – were another matter. It became known that Bub was gunning for Bumpy, and vice-versa. There were a few times when the two came in contact with each other, and both bore the bullet wounds to prove it, but neither managed to permanently get rid of the other.

But then in December of 1932, Bub made a mistake – and it had nothing to do with Bumpy.

In addition to working for Schultz, Bub also worked – and was friends with – real estate entrepreneur Leroy Wilkins; brother to slain club owner Barron Wilkins. Well, Leroy, who was 56, fell in love with a pretty young thing named Daisy. He set her up in a swanky apartment and "kept her," in furs and jewels, which delighted Daisy, but didn't go over well with Daisy's husband, Alonzo Scott. When Scott tried to persuade Daisy to come home, Wilkins asked Bub to talk some sense into the young man.

Bub visited Scott, and told him that Wilkins was willing to pay him $10,000 to forget about Daisy, but Scott refused. Bub left him with a warning – leave Daisy alone. When Daisy told Wilkins that Scott had once again contacted her, Wilkins asked Bub to take care of him.

On December 18th, 1932, Scott was walking along Lenox Avenue when suddenly someone came up from behind him and pinned his arms behind his back. Then Bub, Fritzie Grant, and Malcolm "Blue" Renier appeared. Bub and Fritzie started beating the man, and Blue took out a switchblade and slashed him a few times. Then they hustled him into a waiting car, drove him around for an hour or so – beating him the whole time – and then finally dumped him on the sidewalk in front of Harlem Hospital.

Bub, who by this time was 46, had been arrested more than 40 times, but had been able to beat all but the most minor of raps because witnesses were afraid to identify him. Scott, however, pressed charges and agreed to testify in court.

Bub, Blue, Fritzie, Wilkins, and Wilkins' chauffeur (who was accused of driving the car in which Scott had been taken for a ride) were all arrested. Wilkins and his chauffeur were later released because of lack of evidence against them. The case went to trial in March 1933, and Scott appeared in court swathed in bandages and with cigarette burns dotting his body and his cheeks. The prosecutor told the courtroom that Bub was a henchman for the Dutch Schultz mob, that Fritzie was the trigger man, and Blue was their knife artist. "This is not the case of Alonzo Scott against the dreaded Bub Hewlett's gang," the prosecutor said, "it is the case of the State of New York against this menace of its welfare." In April of 1933 Bub, Fritzie, and Blue were all convicted and sentenced to 2½ to 5 years.

So contrary to all the stories about Bub and Bumpy gunning for each other for the full three years of the war with Dutch Schultz, Bub was out of the picture in just six months.

Most of the men in Bub's gang who were still on the street abandoned the battle against Bumpy after Bub went away, although there were still a few who continued the fight. And then in 1934 Ulysses Rollins – a hotshot from Chicago with family connections in Washington D.C. – made it known that he was now Dutch's top colored henchman, and he was going to take Bumpy down. Bumpy laughed when he heard the news, but he and his crew stayed on the lookout because Rollins' reputation had preceded him into town, and they knew he was dangerous.

Dutch seldom went to Harlem himself, although he did visit one of his spots on Lenox Avenue from time-to-time, but Bumpy was never able to get a bead on the Dutchman – he always traveled with a heavy entourage of bodyguards including Bo and George Weinberg, Lulu Rosencrantz, and Abe Landau. It was mostly Dutch's outside hired help who were on the frontline in Harlem, and Bumpy was frustrated that he was never able to reach out and actually get Dutch in his sights.

Bumpy knew that even if he couldn't personally get to Dutch, there was someone who could. Lucky Luciano. He contacted Luciano in late 1934. From what I understand Bumpy told him about the Hell going on in Harlem. Luciano, of course, knew most of what was going on, but he listened intently as Bumpy filled him in on all of the details. When he finished Luciano said he couldn't get involved but if, hypothetically, he did get involved, he would want to take over the numbers racket in Harlem and put Bumpy on his payroll for say, a thousand dollars a week. Bumpy told him that he was disappointed that he wouldn't get involved, but that if Luciano did, hypothetically, get involved and then try to move against the Harlem bankers that he – Bumpy – would have no choice but to take Luciano on. Luciano laughed, and said that there was no way Bumpy would be able to survive a war against him, and Bumpy smiled and said, "That's the same thing Schultz said. And here I am, three years later, speaking with you."

Luciano was impressed with Bumpy, but still refused to get involved. The two shook hands and left it at that. For the moment.

The war in Harlem continued to wage, and in the summer of 1935 Bumpy and Ulysses finally had a face-to-face confrontation.

Bumpy had started an affair with Helen Lawrenson – the white editor of Vanity Fair – and was taking her to dinner at the Alhambra Bar and Theatre on 126th Street and Seventh Avenue when Bumpy spotted Rollins. He pulled out a knife and jumped on Rollins, and the two men rolled around on the floor for a few moments before finally Bumpy stood up and straightened his tie. Rollins remained on the floor, his face and body badly gashed, and one of his eyeballs hanging from the socket by ligaments. Bumpy calmly stepped over the man, picked up a menu and said he suddenly had a taste for spaghetti and meatballs.

An ambulance was called, and although everyone assumed that Rollins was fatally wounded, he proved just as tough as his reputation had promised. He got out of the hospital that same night, and – his face almost totally covered in bandages – he went looking for Bumpy. He found him at Frank's Restaurant on 125th Street, pulled a gun and shot at Bumpy's head. Maybe it was because he now only had one good eye, but he missed his mark –though barely. The bullet went through Bumpy's hat and hit an innocent woman, killing her. Rollins was hauled off by an off-duty police officer who happened to be at the restaurant. He was eventually convicted and sent to prison. Bumpy never wore a hat again.

Bumpy fervently wanted Schultz dead, and in October 1935 he got his wish. Schultz – along with Rosencrantz, Landau, and Otto Berman – were gunned down at a restaurant in Newark, New Jersey. The hit was ordered by Luciano – but not because of any favor he was trying to do for Bumpy. Schultz had let it be known that he was planning on putting a contract on Special Prosecutor Thomas E. Dewey, and wouldn't listen when the Italian mob said it would bring down too much heat on all of their operations. Rather than letting Schultz hit Dewey, Luciano had Schultz hit.

Schultz didn't die on the spot, though – he lingered on death's bed in Newark City Hospital for twenty hours. Harlem rejoiced when the news got out that Schultz was dying, and Madame Queen – ever the classy lady – sent a telegram to the hospital addressed to Schultz which simply read, "As you sow so shall you reap."

The question now, though, was what was going to happen to the numbers game in Harlem? Was Luciano going to act on the hypothetical he had given Bumpy?

A week after Schultz's death, Bumpy and Luciano met again, this time at Luciano's request – but while Luciano requested the meeting he let Bumpy speak first. Bumpy told him that he did realize that he couldn't win a war against Luciano, but there was still no way he could just sit back and let the numbers racket get taken away from the blacks. But, he said, if Luciano wanted to take over the bankers who had went with Dutch, and offered Bumpy no help in the war against the Dutchman, he wouldn't lose any sleep over a bunch of cowards who'd shown they had no backbone. Luciano nodded, and said that Bumpy was "indeed a smart man, for a nig. . . a negro." but that while he could agree that he wouldn't move on any of the bankers who had stood with Bumpy against Dutch, that any other new bank that opened would have to come under Italian control. Bumpy also wanted to become Luciano's Harlem partner – the mob would attempt to do nothing in Harlem without Bumpy's approval, and without giving Bumpy the opportunity to also wet his beak. The two haggled for hours on the points, with Luciano at one point saying, "Don't you realize I'm doing you a favor? I could kill you right now and just take over everything." Bumpy smiled and told Luciano that he knew that he was too good a businessman to do something like that. When Luciano asked what he meant, Bumpy said that even if he were killed during the meeting he still had men on the street who would carry on the war, and while they might not win they could sure slow down business, just as they had done with Schultz. When Luciano said it would just be a matter of time before they were also wiped out, Bumpy said, "How you gonna know who they all are? You know we niggers all look alike to you guin . . . guys."

Luciano frowned, and said, "Did you almost say 'to you guineas?'"

Bumpy replied, "No. Unless you almost said I'm a smart man for a nigger."

Luciano started laughing, and the two shook hands. The deal was cut.

It wasn't a perfect solution, and not everyone was happy, but at the same time the people of Harlem realized Bumpy had ended the war with no further losses, and had negotiated a peace with honor. And because of that, they were grateful.

And they realized that for the first time a black man had stood up to the white mob instead of just bowing down and going along to get along. And because of that, they were in awe.

Bumpy was now a living legend.

Chapter Six – Hail to the King

Bumpy and his crew could do no wrong in Harlem. Everyone wanted to be their friend, and everybody wanted to do things for them. Bumpy didn't drink, but whenever he went into a bar or nightclub his sodas were on the house. Celebrities would come over and introduce themselves to him. And women were all over him.

But what I think Bumpy loved most was that the Italians soon found out that the deal they cut was a deal they had to live up to. For instance, when they decided to muscle their way into a numbers bank that was supposed to be off limits, they ran up against Bumpy. No, another war wasn't declared. But when the banker complained to Bumpy, Bumpy called a meeting of all the numbers bankers, controllers and number runners at the 369th Armory at Fifth Avenue and 143rd Street. The meeting only lasted two hours, but when they left everyone had their marching orders. A full fifty percent of the runners working for the Italian controlled banks called in sick the following morning, and the ones who reported to work only brought in a tenth of their usual take. Bumpy had called for a work slow down. It only took two days before Bumpy was contacted by the one of Luciano's men and told that "the boss" wanted to see him. Bumpy went to Luciano's suite at the Waldorf-Astoria that afternoon.

"So, what's been going on uptown?" Lucky asked him after they exchanged pleasantries.

"Nothing new," Bumpy answered.

"Is that so? I hear the money's not been so good lately."

"Really? I'm sorry to hear you say that," Bumpy said innocently. "Anything I can do to help?"

Luciano eyeballed him for a moment, then said, "We're both businessmen, let's lay our cards on the table. You got a problem, you come to me and I straighten it out. I'm the boss. Remember that?"

Bumpy leaned forward. "We had a deal. You don't move against any of the independent bankers."

Luciano nodded. "This man you're talking about, he owes us money. The way it's figured if he owes us, we own him. Understand?"

Bumpy shook his head. "No, I don't understand. If you had a problem with one of my people then why didn't you come to me? In Harlem, I'm the boss. Remember that?"

"You? Now you're the boss?"

"In Harlem, yes. You may control the rest of New York, and I respect that. I would never make a move against one of your friends. I give you that respect. You're a man worthy of that respect." Bumpy waited a moment for his compliment to sink in before adding, "But I'm a man also worthy of respect."

"I recognize that, Bumpy. And you know I'm a man who gives respect. Don't matter to me if they're a Jew, a Mick, or a Negro. We all want to make some money, eh? Live and let live."

"Exactly."

It took another thirty minutes, but they finally worked it out – Lucky's people were going to lay off Bumpy's friend's bank, but Bumpy was going to make sure the banker paid what he owed them, and at a much steeper interest rate.

Bumpy was about to leave when he noticed a chessboard set up on one of the tables in the suite. "You play, huh?"

Luciano looked at him in surprise. "Yeah. You?" Then he paused. "Never mind, I should have figured that."

"What do you mean?"

"You're a man who always seems to have his moves planned two steps ahead."

Bumpy laughed. "So do you."

"Me?" Luciano grinned. "Nah. I plan four or five moves ahead."

"Is that right? You got time for a game?"

Bumpy won the first match, and Lucky won the next. The next two games they played to a draw. It became a regular thing with them. They always got together at least once a week to play chess. I don't suppose you'd ever say they became close friends, but they had genuine fondness for each other. Lucky even came to Harlem a couple of times to play at Bumpy's favorite spot – in front of the YMCA on 135th Street which had just opened a couple of years before.

Their friendly, but very competitive, chess games continued until 1936 when Lucky got sent up to prison.

Bumpy told me that he knew one of the reasons Lucky agreed to abide by the deal they had struck in 1935 was because Luciano was feeling some real heat from Special Prosecutor Thomas Dewey, the same guy who went after Schultz for tax evasion. Luciano didn't need the publicity that another war would bring, no matter who he thought would be the victor. In June 1936 Dewey managed to convict Luciano on a compulsory prostitution charge. Most of the men in the gangster life knew it was a frame-up, but it didn't matter. Luciano was sentenced to thirty years and sent to Dannemora.

Luciano might not have had anything to do with prostitution, but the same couldn't be said for Bumpy.

He never considered himself a pimp because he didn't go out and recruit prostitutes, but if a working girl wanted protection without hooking up with one of those gorilla pimps who'd beat them and take all their money Bumpy was more than willing to help them out – for a cut of their nightly take. And when a girl held out on him he wouldn't beat them up, but he'd do things like go to their apartment and cut up all their clothes or something. He didn't really have it in him to strong arm a woman. But he didn't have any real problems, because the girls were happy to have someone looking after them that didn't demand all their money. And if they were known as one of Bumpy's girls they knew no one in the street would bother them.

Bumpy had a close relationship with a few of the women, and he was particularly fond of one of them – a Jewish prostitute named Yetta Goldberg.

He also had an ongoing relationship with Helen Lawrenson, an editor over at the prestigious magazine Vanity Fair. Helen was one of those downtown white women who loved coming up to Harlem to rub elbows with the 'real bad guys,' and when someone pointed out Bumpy to her, and told her of his reputation, she couldn't wait to get in his face. She loved going around Harlem on Bumpy's arm, and she used to brag to all her friends that she was a gangster's moll. She even devoted a chapter to him in her memoir, *Stranger at the Party*. In it she talks about all the gifts that Bumpy gave her. I don't know all about that, but I do know she was giving him money and gifts, because he still had a couple of diamond rings she gave when I met him in 1948. In fact, I met Helen Lawrenson in 1948 shortly after Bumpy came out of prison. Most white folks had quit partying in Harlem by then, but when she heard Bumpy was home she hurried her butt up there to see him. I was with him. She walked into the Alhambra

Theater and walked straight to our table. At first Bumpy seemed both surprised and happy to see her. But then when he introduced us instead of saying hello she looked me up and down and said, "Well, Bumpy, I see it didn't take you long to get back to your old tricks. One of your top girls, or is she new on the scene?"

My mouth dropped open, but before I could say anything Bumpy gave her a cold stare and said, "Mayme's my woman."

At which point she giggled and said, "Aren't we all?"

Well why did she say that? Bumpy stood up and said, "Helen, you need to leave. And don't let me see you uptown again."

This time it was Helen's mouth that dropped open. "Bumpy, I was just . . ."

He cut her off. "You ain't hear me good?"

She didn't say another word. She just turned on her heels and walked out. I never saw her again.

But that was in 1948.

Getting back to 1935, like I said, they definitely had a thing going. But he had a lot things going with various women; both black and white.

By this time all of Bumpy's sisters – including Marjorie – were falling all over themselves to be close to Bumpy because of the bragging rights he afforded them. If they casually mentioned they were related to Bumpy they could go into any restaurant or club in Harlem and never be presented a check. Everyone treated them like queens because everyone wanted to get in good with Bumpy.

Well one day, in 1935, Bumpy showed up at Genevieve's door with a baby in his arms.

"Ginny," he said as he stepped in the apartment. "This is my daughter. I need you take care of her."

"Your daughter?" Ginny took a good look at the infant. "Bumpy this is a white baby!"

"How she gonna be a white baby when I just said I'm her father?"

"Well, who's her mother?" Ginny asked.

"Don't worry about it."

"What do you mean don't worry about it?" Ginny demanded. "I know she's white whoever she is. What you doing bringing some white or half-white baby to my door talking about you need me to take care of it?"

"Look, her name is Elease and she's an angel. Doesn't hardly cry or anything," Bumpy said as he tried to hand the baby off to Genevieve, "All that matters is the mother can't take care of her so I need you to do it."

"I ain't taking care of no baby. You named her after Elease, you carry the child down to Charleston and let Elease take care of her," Genevieve snapped at him.

"I don't want my baby that far from me," Bumpy said.

"You shoulda thought about all that before you knocked some white woman up."

"Ginny, stop it," Bumpy said impatiently. "Look, what you make at your job? Ten, twelve dollars a week? I'll give you twenty-five a week and take care of all her expenses."

Genevieve didn't have a problem taking care of the baby then.

Bumpy never did say who Elease's mother was. He would never even tell Elease when she grew up. Said he had promised the mother he'd never tell, and it didn't matter anyway because all Elease needed was him. When she went to get her birth certificate years later it said that she was born in New Jersey and her mother's name was Helen Morgan. When she asked

Bumpy how she could find Helen Morgan he said it was a made-up name that her mother gave the hospital.

I always thought it was wrong for Elease never to know who her mother was, but Bumpy said he made the promise, and he was sticking to it. The mother kept her part of the promise by giving him the baby instead of getting rid of it, and he was sticking to his part. And he always left it just at that.

As for whatever happened to Madame Stephanie St. Clair, well she was quite upset with Bumpy. Not because of the peace he negotiated – she was as glad as anyone that the war was finally over – but because after it was over he opened his own numbers bank instead of coming back to work for her. She figured with his new found fame and adoration, she would be the most acclaimed numbers banker in Harlem with him and his crew behind her. For his part, he figured he could more money banking numbers himself rather than just working for a banker.

Then in 1936 she actually got married! To the very dashing and flamboyant Sufi Abdul Hamid. History gives credit to Adam Clayton Powell, Jr. for forcing the white department stores in Harlem to hire blacks, but it was actually Hamid, who came to New York in 1932, who was actually the first one to organize boycotts and picket outside the stores. He was demonized for his efforts – the New York papers nicknamed him the "Black Hitler," but he ignored them and kept up his activities. While Madame Queen was standing on a soapbox on 125th Street and Seventh Avenue berating blacks not to give their number business to Dutch Schultz, Hamid was on a soapbox on the opposite corner yelling through a megaphone, "If you can't work there, you shouldn't buy there," referring to the stores. Hamid, like Madame Queen, wore a turban, and also sported a long flowing cape, a wide leather belt, and shiny black military boots. The two of them made quite a pair.

Bumpy, and a number of Harlemites gave generously to Hamid's campaign, but none as generously as Madame Queen, who was only just beginning to financially recover from the money she lost during the Dutch Schultz reign. Maybe that's why she flew off the handle when she found that Hamid was having an affair. Instead of asking for a divorce, she decided to settle things in her own special way. So, she took a .38 and plugged two nice size holes into Hamid. He lived, but she was sentenced to ten years in prison for attempted murder. When she got out she moved into a mansion in Long Island, never again getting into the numbers business. She died in December 1969; far from broke, I might add. As for Hamid, he married the woman with whom he was having the affair, but died in an airplane crash over Long Island in 1938.

But Madame Queen wasn't the only one to get arrested in 1937.

New York Charlie was a well-known pimp around Harlem – the type who used to gorilla prostitutes to make them work for him. In other words, he'd pick out a girl and beat her until she agreed to have him as her pimp. Well, he decided to gorilla one of the girls whom Bumpy was protecting. And one that he knew that Bumpy was protecting! When Bumpy found out he went looking for New York Charlie and sliced him up pretty bad. As far as Bumpy was concerned it was nothing personal, New York Charlie just had to be put in his place. So after the knife assault Bumpy went to Smalls Paradise and was having dinner with friends when a police officer came in and told him that he was under arrest. When Bumpy asked why, the officer said that New York Charlie had identified him as the person who landed him in the hospital. Bumpy told the officer

110

there had to be some mistake, and asked to be brought to the hospital so that New York Charlie could admit his error. Well, when they got to Sydenham Hospital, New York Charlie was being prepped to go into the operating room. To Bumpy's surprise, the pimp growled to the police, "Yeah, that's the motherfucker who cut me up." Bumpy immediately jumped on New York Charlie and started choking him while he lay on the hospital gurney. The police had to beat Bumpy into unconsciousness with their nightsticks before he would release the man's throat.

Bumpy was sentenced to 10 years for felonious assault, and off he went to Dannemora.

Chapter Seven – Drop Me Off In Harlem

It was 1947 -- Bumpy was free and, as he later told me, he was pissed.

He stood outside the gate of Dannemora in Clinton, New York and started walking toward the bus that would take him home to Harlem, ignoring the 1947 red Cadillac slowly cruising in the street next to him, and the driver inside trying to get his attention.

"Bumpy!" Obadiah Green, shouted out the car window, "Would you get your ashy black ass in this car?"

"Man," Bumpy finally said in a loud growl, "You don't want me to get in, because if I do I'm gonna strangle you with my bare hands, and I just got out of prison. I want to at least get one home-cooked meal before I get sent back."

"Nigger, what the hell are you talking about?" Obadiah asked as he pulled the car over and opened the door.

"Don't get out that car!" Bumpy warned.

"What? What you talking about?"

"I said, don't get out the car," Bumpy said. "because if you do, I promise I'm going to kill you."

"Huh?" Obadiah told me he hesitated, but then figured Bumpy was making some kind of a joke, so he just gave a laugh and said, "Man, I just drove ten hours from Harlem to pick you up and you talking about killing me?"

"Yeah, I'm talking about killing you dead." Bumpy pointed his index finger at Obadiah and cocked his thumb back as if pulling the trigger of a gun. "You, Nat, Finley, Georgie, Ritchie, Junie . . . the whole lot of you. You no good bunch of dirty hypocritical bastards."

"Man, what are you talking about?" Obadiah swung one of his feet outside of the car, but when he saw the glint in Bumpy's eyes he swung it back inside and slammed the door shut.

"Can we talk about this?" Obadiah asked through the open window. "Just tell me what you're so mad about."

"Go to Hell," Bumpy said as he once again started walking toward the bus station.

"You mad 'cause we ain't take care of New York Charlie?" Obadiah started as he drove next to Bumpy. "Man, you know we wanted to, but you was the one told us to lay off."

"Fuck New York Charlie. I told y'all I'll take care of him myself."

"Then, what's the matter?"

Bumpy stooped, picked up a rock, and aimed it at Obadiah's head, but before he could throw it, the red Cadillac sped off.

It might have taken Obadiah ten hours to get from Harlem to Dannemora, but to hear him tell it, he made it back to Harlem in only eight. And soon as he got back, he told me, he called up Dickie Wells and told him what happened.

Dickie Wells was a well-respected man around Harlem, an old friend of Bumpy's, and one of the few who knew how to handle him. Dickie had always acted as peacemaker, and he was certainly needed that day.

When Bumpy got off the bus at the George Washington Bus Terminal, Dickie was sitting in a big black Lincoln waiting on him.

"I need a piece," Bumpy said as he got in the car.

"Yeah, hello to you, too, nigger," Dickie said as he started the car and pulled off. "What kind of piece you looking at?"

113

"A .35 will do nicely," Bumpy replied, staring stonily out the window.

Dickie told me he nodded, waiting for Bumpy to continue, but after a few minutes of silence he finally broke down and asked, "And what you need the piece for?"

"I'ma shoot Junie and them," Bumpy said simply.

"Oh, okay, then." Dickie knew Bumpy well -- well enough to know that if he started arguing with him that Bumpy would just become more stubborn and determined. He drove a few more blocks before nonchalantly asking, "Shoot them dead?"

Bumpy hesitated, then said, "Naw, maybe just shoot them in the foot or some shit." He thought about it some more for a moment, then said, "Maybe just pistol whip their asses. But I'ma do something."

"Pistol whipping. That should work. What they do?"

Bumpy slammed his fist down on the dashboard, hard. "Man, they been fucking over me for the last year."

"You shitting me. I thought those were your ace boon coons."

"Yeah, I thought so, too. We been through a lot of shit together, you know that," Bumpy said. "And the first nine years I was gone they was sending me my cut and shit, like promised, but all of a sudden the money got funny. I'm only been getting two hundred bucks a month. And I had to send a hundred of that to my sister to take care of my daughter."

"Naw, that shit is wrong!" Dickie told me he all but shouted.

"Hell, yeah, it's wrong. Them niggers was making big bucks. I set Junie up with a numbers bank before I left, and I know he was raking in at least four

114

thousand a week offa that. And I helped Finley get on the big circuit, and Nat, hell, you know good as me what Nat be doing. You gonna tell me my cut weren't but no two hundred bucks a month? Man, fuck a pistol whipping. I'ma be shooting me some niggers today."

Dickie pulled over to the sidewalk, tires squealing. He turned in the driver's seat to face Bumpy. "Naw, man. I'm saying that's wrong. They was sending you a whole helluva lot more than two hundred a month. They was sending you a hunnert a piece, man. That's six hunnert, right? And I gave them five hundred myself to send to you a couple of months ago cause I hit on your number so I figured I'd send a little extra good cheer."

"I ain't get no five hundred dollars from you."

"Look," Dickie told him, "We had a party at the Rhythm Club and I gave Junie five hundred dollars from the door to send you and I saw him, myself, put it in an envelope and give it to Hoss to bring you on his next visit. Didn't Hoss come see you a couple of months ago?"

"Yeah," Bumpy said slowly. "Hoss came up a couple of months ago, with a whole seventy-five from the crew. He put in an extra hunnert out his own pocket to help me tide over."

"Well, that nigger done lied to you, and I can bear witness to that," Dickie said firmly.

"Ain't that some shit? I'm gonna fucking kill Hoss." Bumpy started shouting. "That greasy, low-life, pigfoot eating, no-good thieving motherfucker."

"Yeah, Hoss ain't shit if he shorted you, man. But I bet Junie and them ain't know nothing about it. Hell, they gonna probably wanna kill his ass, too, when they find out he been taking their paper and pocketing it. Especially that tight-ass Finley. Junie and Nat had to practically pull a gun on that nigger every month for him to ante up his cut."

"Yeah, well, a leopard don't change his spots, Finley's always been like that. But wait until I get that fucking Hoss. I'm a beat him to a pulp."

"I don't blame you no one bit. But first I'ma take you over to my house, and have my mother fix you some food. Not that it looks like you been hurting for any meals, though. You done put on a few pounds."

Later that night, Dickie told Bumpy he had had to stop over to Harris' Bar on 132nd Street and Seventh, to pick up money someone owed him and he wanted Bumpy to ride along in case the guy wanted to make trouble. But when they got there the place was dark, and the doors were locked. It was only two a.m., and Harris' stayed open until four, so Bumpy told me he couldn't figure out what the heck was going on. Dickie told him there was only one way to find out, so he gave a quick couple raps on the glass door. A bartender came over and let them in the darkened bar, and Bumpy said he had only taken a couple of steps in when someone turned on the light.

"Surprise!" two hundred voices yelled in unison. Bumpy didn't have heart trouble at that point, but he told me he swore he near had a heart attack. There crowded in that small bar was darn near everyone he knew, and a good fifty or so people he didn't. Suddenly, Bumpy said, the jukebox was blaring Duke Ellington's "Drop Me Off in Harlem," which he had recorded about a decade earlier. Duke had written the music for the song, but the lyrics were actually written by a white newspaper columnist for the New York Daily News named Nick Kenny. Nick had hailed a cab and offered Duke a ride. When he asked Duke where he was going, Duke climbed into the taxi and said simply, Harlem. When Nick pressed him for an exact location,

Duke replied, "Man, any old place in Harlem." A couple of nights later Nick brought Duke the lyrics, and Duke recorded it in 1933. It got a new life because of that Eddie Murphy and Richard Pryor movie, "Harlem Nights," a very good movie, by the way.

Any how, the juke box was blasting, and the joint was jumping, and everyone was crowding around Bumpy slapping him on his back and welcoming him home as they handed him envelopes filled with money; the traditional "walking around money" given to sporting men when they got out the joint so they could quickly get on their feet and back in business.

"Come here, boy, and let me take a look at you," boomed a voice from behind him. Bumpy turned around and there stood Johnny Walker, one of the number bankers who stood with Bumpy during the Dutch Schultz war in the early thirties.

"Man, if you ain't a sight for sore eyes," Johnny Walker said, pulling Bumpy into a hug. "You done put on some weight, though. You musta taken a liking to that prison food."

"I wasn't about to eat that slop they served up there," Bumpy told me he answered. "But I had me some helluva good Italian food, fried calamari, pasta . . ."

"Don't tell me you turned into a wop while you was away!" Johnny Walker started laughing.

"Naw, but the made men there had it good, having all their food shipped in, and cooking it themselves. And after I helped Lucky out with a certain little situation I was invited to all the meals," Bumpy said with a grin. "And them greaseballs can cook their asses off."

"You helped Lucky Luciano outta what situation?" Johnny Walker asked him. "Wait, hold on, first I wanna introduce you to someone," Johnny

Walker said as a young man and woman walked up. "Bumpy, this is Chink Cunningham. And this is his wife, Evelyn."

"How do you do?" Bumpy said addressing Evelyn first. "It's a pleasure to meet you."

Evelyn smiled and extended her hand, saying the pleasure was hers, but Bumpy said he got the distinct feeling that the woman was uncomfortable; and maybe had already formed an unfavorable impression of him. That always bothered Bumpy, because he grew to really like and admire Evelyn Cunningham. She was a tall woman, with red hair, and dressed very tastefully, and her sophistication was obvious, and not at all fake. She was a reporter for the old Negro newspaper, The Pittsburgh Courier, but based in Harlem, and smart as hell. But Evelyn was always kind of aloof to Bumpy, even though he and Chink became good friends.

Now talk about a love affair? That's what Evelyn and Chink had. I don't know exactly when they got married, but the whole time they were together they acted like they was still on their honeymoon. He used to buy her minks and cars, and fly her from Pittsburgh to Harlem every weekend so they could spend time together before she got the permanent position in Harlem. That man loved himself some Evelyn, and it seemed like she loved him that much more. I think I remember Bumpy telling me they was childhood sweethearts. Chink was Johnny Walker's protégé, and was bringing in big money in the numbers business, so you would have thought they made an odd pair, because Evelyn traveled in all the right circles, if you know what I mean. She even became a bigwig in New York politics, and worked for the mayor, I think. But like I said, she loved herself some Chink. Even after they were divorced, and she went on to marry a couple of other men she kept his last name. Evelyn Cunningham.

Yep, that's still her name today. Last I heard she was living on Riverside Drive.

"So, Bumpy, what are your plans? You gonna get back into action?" Johnny Walker asked after he made the introductions.

Bumpy told me that Evelyn cleared her throat, and then said, "If you gentlemen are going to talk business I think I'll just go ahead and sit and finish my drink."

Chink said, "Excuse me for a moment," and then took Evelyn's hand and escorted her back to their table. Bumpy said he was just bowled over because he had never seen a couple so much in love. Of course, you understand, this was before he met me.

"I wanted you to meet Chink because he's going to take over from me some day. The kid's smart. Real smart," Johnny Walker said as Chink and Evelyn walked away. "I've known him since he was a teenager. He grew up in Sugar Hill. Keep your eye on him. The man's going places."

"Well, if he's your man then he's my man," Bumpy said. "I'll look out for him and make sure he doesn't get into any trouble."

"Naw, man, you don't have to worry about Chink," Johnny Walker said. "He's not the get-into-trouble kind of guy."

When Chink returned, he, Johnny Walker and Bumpy got down to business -- specifically talking about the number business.

"I'm planning on swinging back into action in a couple of weeks, I wanna scope out the landscape some, but you know my main area is 135th Street, so I'm gonna see what I can do over there," Bumpy told the men. "If you guys want to join up . . ."

Johnny Walker waved his hand and said, no. "We're good, man. We got Sugar Hill . . ."

"Yeah, I ain't planning on moving in on your territory, you know that."

"Man, you know I know you ain't like that. But like I said, we're good. But," Johnny Walker gave Chink a look, and the young man pulled a bulging white envelope out of his inside suit pocket, "we wanna make sure you're good, too." He took the envelope from Chink and handed it to Bumpy. "Here's a little something to start up your bank, plus a little walking around money."

"I'ma need at least five thousand to start the bank, just in case I get some big hits the first couple of weeks."

Johnny Walker pointed to the envelope. "You covered in there for a couple of months."

"Solid," Bumpy said as he slid the envelope in his pocket with the twenty or so already there.

Bumpy said he knew Johnny Walker was going to give him something, but he had no idea that the man was willing to part with so much cash. "You two must really be doing good."

"I told you we was doing good," Johnny Walker said.

And he must have been, because Bumpy told me later that one envelope contained twenty thousand dollars. Keep in mind this was in 1947, so that would be about the equivalent of maybe one hundred thousand these days. Bumpy also told me that he found out later that Johnny Walker was pulling in $90,000 a month from his numbers bank. He really was doing good.

Bumpy said he was there at Harris' for about a half hour before Junie, Nat, Finley, Obadiah, Ritchie and Six-n-Eight walked in the bar.

"Where y'all niggers been?" Bumpy greeted them. "I thought y'all would be the first people here at the party."

"We was looking for that no-good nigger, Hoss. Someone told us he was holed up in Brooklyn so we went looking for him. We ain't find him, but we will," Finley grumbled as he took a seat at the bar. "That nigger's gonna give me back my money."

"How's it your money when you gave it to him to give it to me?" Bumpy asked.

"He ain't give it to you so it's mine again. And I plan on getting it back," Finley said with a snarl. "You got a problem with that."

"Listen to Finley talking shit," Junie said as he hugged Bumpy. "How you doing, man?"

"I'm doing fine, now," Bumpy said patting his pocket.

"I know we getting a cut of that," Finley said, eying the bulge.

"Yeah, I'll give you a cut alright, but it ain't gonna be of no money," Bumpy answered.

"Hey, Finley. You want Hoss, there he goes," Nat said nodding his head at a man sitting at the bar.

Bumpy turned, expecting to find Hoss Steele, and instead there was another Hoss seated at the bar across from them. Horace "Hoss" Cartwright. And next to him was Fess Taylor.

"Who let those motherfuckers in here?" Bumpy asked as he glared at the men.

"Don't know," Nat said. "But Fess has really come up big since you been gone. Dealing with the Italians, and shit. There's a lot of money to be made selling dope."

"Yeah," Bumpy said, "From what I understand, you should know."

Nat shrugged. "I ain't doing nothing real big, just a little here and there when the opportunity presents itself."

121

"Just don't bring that shit around me," Bumpy said. "Who's that red nigger sitting next to them?"

"Him? That's Red Dillard Morrison. He's new on the scene," Obadiah answered. "He's supposed to be Fess' right hand man."

"I thought Horace was Fess' guy," Bumpy said.

"He still is, but Fess really likes Red. Treats him like a son."

Bumpy said Red must have sensed they were talking about him because he suddenly looked up and shone a pearly white smile in their direction, then got up and walked over to them.

"How you doing, Bumpy?" Red said sticking out his hand.

Bumpy said he was about to ignore the man, but just then he looked over and saw that Fess and Horace were snarling and looking at Red as if they'd been betrayed. Bumpy shook the man's hand just to piss them off.

"I've heard a lot about you," Red said. "Welcome back."

"Thanks."

Bumpy said Red stood there for a moment, like he was hoping Bumpy would continue talking, but Bumpy just turned around and started talking to Junie and them again.

"Well, I guess I'll be seeing you around," Red said, then strolled back over to his seat. Bumpy said he watched as Fess and Horace lit into him, but Red seemed to just shrug them off.

"He's got a lot of nerve, I'll say that about him," Bumpy said to Junie and them. "But I don't like him. That nigger thinks he's pretty."

Now let me say right now that is exactly what Red thought, and he was right. Lord help me for saying it, but Red Dillard Morrison was the best looking man

I've ever set eyes on. I met him just a few months after Bumpy, and just looking at him 'bout took my breath away. He was about 6-feet tall, with a slim athletic build, and had the easy, yet powerful stride of a panther. He was light-skinned, kinda reddish in tone, with dark red hair. His cheekbones were so high they almost met his dark piercing eyes. While Bumpy always wore his hair natural, back in the thirties and forties a lot of black men processed their hair. But while most wore it straight back like Duke Ellington and Cab Calloway, Red wore his hair in a Marcel – processed but with a wave through it; like Nat King Cole, only prettier.

And oh, that man could dress. I mean, Bumpy could dress, don't get me wrong, but Red looked like clothes were invented just to adorn his body. The man was sharp as a tack. I'm telling you he was pretty! It seemed the angels sent him down just to let people know what a handsome man was supposed to look like.

Or maybe it was the Devil that sent him up from hell to punish women, because Red was as mean as he was pretty. While Red dealt dope and hung around Fess and Horace Cartwright, he made most of his money as a pimp. He pulled both black and white prostitutes, and none of the frumpy looking types – Red's women were beautiful, and they kept him in fancy cars and expensive clothes. And in return he treated them like dirt.

One time one of his girls came up short, and he beat her so bad outside of Minton's Playhouse on 118th Street that he knocked out almost all of her upper teeth. He went back inside the club and joked that now maybe she could specialize in "gumming dick." That's the kind of guy Red was.

Red was mean, handsome, and ambitious as hell. Seems I remember hearing he was from North

Carolina, though born in Alabama. He'd moved into Harlem while Bumpy was away in Dannemora, and hooked up with Fess Taylor shortly afterward. But he'd heard about Bumpy, and he was hedging his bets. I'm pretty sure if he thought he could get in with Bumpy he woulda dropped Fess like a hot potato. That's why he went up and introduced himself that night Bumpy came home; even though he had to know it would piss Fess off. But Bumpy never really took to Red, though he did admire the man's spunk. Red wasn't one of those men pretending to be tough, he really was.

Minton's Playhouse on 118th Street near St. Nicholas Avenue was Red's favorite hangout spot. Minton's was the favorite hangout for a lotta guys back then in the late forties and early fifties – not just the sporting men, but also jazz musicians including Thelonius Monk, Charlie Mingus, Charlie "Yardbird" Parker, and Dizzy Gillespie. In fact, they say Minton's was the place where be-bop jazz was born. The Monday Night Jam sessions there were legendary, and musicians from all over the city would come to hear the masters play.

Well, about 4:30 a.m on a Saturday, when most of the crowd was gone and the manager was counting up the receipts, three men sporting .38's burst through the door and ordered everyone to get to the floor. Like I said, most of the crowd had already gone home, but Red was there, along with about a dozen other folks, but everyone hit the floor like ordered and in a hurry. One of the gunmen told the manager to hand over the money, and when the guy groaned and said something like, "Oh man," as he turned over the dough the gunman started pistol whipping him.

Now, first off, it was wrong for them guys to even think about robbing Minton's. It was a Harlem institution, like Small's Paradise, and Well's

124

Bumpy in Alcatraz

Mayme Johnson 1955

Bumpy & Flash Walker in 1950. Flash later turned on Bumpy and testified against him in a drug trial which sent Bumpy to prison for 10 years

Bumpy and Mayme at Bear Mountain 1966

Bumpy at Margaret's 14th Birthday Party 1964

Billie Holiday – wearing the expensive jade earrings her abusive boyfriend, John Levy, later sold to Bumpy for $50

Casper Holstein – One of the richest number bankers in Harlem during the 1920s. A native of the Virgin Islands, Holstein was a major benefactor of the Harlem Renaissance.

Bill "Bojangles" Robinson caught in an unguarded moment in 1918. According to Bumpy, Robinson was quite a fighter in his day.

Bub Hewlett (left) in 1918 Harlem. Bub was known as one of the first of "Harlem's Bad Men" -- men who stood up against thugs brought in by white shopowners to stop African-Americans from opening their own businesses.

Bub Hewlett at the Lenox Lounge in 1948. The Lenox Lounge, located on Lenox Avenue near 125th Streets, is one of the few clubs around in Bumpy and Bub's day which still operates today.

Bumpy's childhood friend, Junie Byrd (on the right). Bumpy died in his arms at Wells Restaurant in 1968

127

Bumpy's Granddaughter
Margaret Johnson

Bumpy's great grandson
Anthony Hatcher Johnson

Henry "Perk" Perkins in front of his club, Perks Cuisine, located at 123rd Street and Manhattan Avenue.

Mayme Johnson – 2007

Bumpy (on the left) outside the Federal Courthouse during his 1950's trial.

Restaurant. And the owner, a musician named Henry Minton, was well-known and liked in Harlem, even though he wasn't really a sporting man like Eddie Smalls or Dickie Wells.

Second, it's one thing to rob a spot -- most of the people lying there on the floor had robbed their share of joints -- but it was simply bad manners to pistol whip someone who was turning over the money like asked just because he said, "Oh, man," while doing it.

Red was lying on the floor with the dozen or so other people, but he managed to edge up to the gunman pistol whipping the manager, and pulled the man's pants cuff so hard the guy fell to the ground with his gun in his hand. Red punched him in the face before he could scramble back up, and the guy let loose of the gun. Before Red could grab it, another one of the gunmen pulled Red up by the collar and put his gun in Red's face. Red reached behind him and grabbed a bottle of whiskey on the bar and smashed the guy in the face, then used the broken bottle to slash his throat.

By now, all of the men who'd been lying on the floor were up, and they overpowered the third gunman before he could get off a shot. They locked the doors and beat up on those guys for more than an hour before hustling them in a car and throwing them out on a deserted street to die. The incident didn't make the papers, but the people who knew just knew. And if there was any doubt before there was no doubt afterward, Red Dillard Morrison was one tough character.

But let me finish telling you about that night at Harris' Bar when Bumpy first got out. Shortly after Red got back to his seat, who should walk up but Hoss Steele.

"Man, I oughtta kick your ass," Bumpy said in a growl.

"Why?" Hoss said innocently.

"For not giving me my money," Bumpy answered.

"What money?"

"The money we gave you to give Bumpy, nigger," Finley answered. "And I want mine back."

Hoss just laughed and said, "Man, y'all shoulda known better than to give me money and think I'ma turn it loose. Shit. All y'all know me better than that."

Bumpy looked at him, and Finley later told me they thought he was gonna haul off and beat the shit outta Hoss, but all of a sudden he just waved his hand and said, "Fuck it. Like he said, y'all shoulda known better." I guess he wasn't in the mood to fight about money with all the cash he knew he had in them envelopes. Then he raised up his glass of ginger ale and toasted Hoss. "You my man, and you'll always be my man. And when we meet up in Hell, I'm kicking hot ashes on you, motherfucker."

"Fuck waiting until we get to Hell, I want my money now," Finley said.

Bumpy let his crew argue out and then turned back to continue to try talking Johnny Walker and Chink into going into the number business with him.

"Man," Junie Byrd interrupted. "Things ain't like they used to be, Bumpy. The Italians got things all tied up now. They might not even let you open a spot."

Bumpy swung around to face him. "*Let* me open up a spot? Since when I need permission from a greaseball to open a spot?"

"Like I said, things got different. Nowadays no one opens a spot unless it's sanctioned by the Italians up on the East Side," Junie answered.

Bumpy turned to Johnny Walker. "Tell me, he's lying."

But Johnny Walker told him what Junie Byrd said was right. He told Bumpy that even he had to kick some money up to the Italians. "Not like what Dutch Schultz was trying to pull; it ain't a whole lot. I go ahead and give them their taste to leave me alone."

"You want me to take care of that for you?" Bumpy asked him.

"Man, you just worry about taking care of yourself," Johnny Walker said, slapping Bumpy on the back. I'll be seeing you around."

A few days later Bumpy went up to the East Side to meet with Joey A., who some of you might know as Joe Adonis. Joey A. had been down with Lucky Luciano from way back in the day, and now that Lucky was deported to Italy, Joe was like an acting manager of his operations.

Bumpy didn't care much for Joey A., he considered him vain and conceited, and said the man couldn't pass a mirror without stopping and primping. Still, as concerned as Joey A. was with his looks, he did know how to take care of business – although he was always very careful to never actually get his hands dirty. And he was also loyal -- Joey A. was one of the few guys besides Frank Costello, Thomas Luchese, Meyer Lansky Albert Anastasia, whom Lucky could depend on while he was in the joint to carry out orders and carry them out right.

There was no way that Joey A., or any of the Italians, were coming to Bumpy's homecoming party at Harris' Bar, but he reached out to Bumpy the next day to let him know he had something for him. Bumpy went out to meet him, expecting a big fat envelope, and he wasn't disappointed. But not only did Joey A. give him six thousand dollars, he also handed over a set of car keys for a brand new 1947 black Lincoln Continental.

"Nice," Bumpy later told me he told Joey A., "but I prefer Cadillacs."

"No problem," Joey A. said. "Take the Lincoln now, I'll replace with it a Cadillac in a couple of days."

Bumpy turned him down, explaining he had to get a new drivers license anyway. Then he thanked him for the car and the money. "This is going to come in handy, cause I'm going to be swinging back in action in a couple of days."

"Yeah? That's nice. What kinda action you talking about?"

"Same kind of action I was in before I went up. I'm opening up a bank."

Joey A. looked at him for a moment, then said, quietly, "You got the okay for that, Bumpy?"

"What kind of okay you talking about?"

"From our friends. You talked this over with our friends?"

"Man," Bumpy said standing up, "I don't need to talk it over with nobody. I'm going back in business for myself like always."

Joey A. shrugged and said, "I'll set up a meeting and you come and talk. We'll see what happens."

Bumpy got a call later that evening, and the next day he, Nat, Junie Byrd, Hoss Steele, and Steve Mitchell went to meet with the Italians at the Palma Boys Social Club on 115th Street near Pleasant Avenue on the East Side of Harlem. Bumpy told me he didn't think there'd be any trouble, but he wasn't taking any chances, which is why him and his crew were all strapped. He knew they'd be outnumbered, but since there was so many of them he figured the Italians wouldn't try anything there in the social club – if the meeting didn't go the way they'd want they'd probably try and put the finger on them later but they wouldn't want an all-out shoot out in their club.

Bumpy and his crew walked in and there was a grand round of back slapping and hugs and kissing on the cheeks and then the men all sat down to take care of business. There were about six Italians – including Joey A. – around the table, along with Bumpy and his men.

"We hear you wanna get back in the business, and we wanna help," Anthony "Fat Tony" Salerno said graciously. "You know we always liked you, and we know you're a man worthy of respect. What's it you thinking of doin'?"

"Well, I thank you for your gracious offer of help, and I also thank you for the gifts you've already given me," Bumpy said in just as gracious a tone, "but I don't want to impose on our friendship, you've already done so much. I'm just going to reopen my numbers bank on 135th Street so I can take care of myself."

"Ah, but my friend, that won't be so easy as that," Fat Tony said, his voice taking on a more menacing tone..

"Yeah? Seems to me it should be pretty easy."

"Well, I'm sure you know things have changed since you been gone. That's the way things go. Time goes on, things change. You wanna open up a spot on 135th Street? Fine. We'd be glad to let you do that. But you gotta understand. You run the spot, but you bank your numbers through us." Fat Tony smiled. "You know we gonna give you a good cut. You're a man who's earned our respect."

"Then I expect you to respect the deal that was cut before I left," Bumpy said. "I run my own business with no interference from anyone."

"That deal was cut with some friends who are no longer running things," Fat Tony said. "Like I said, time goes on, things change. You wanna do business, you do business through us."

"I had a deal, and as far as I'm concerned the deal is still on the table."

"The people at the head of the table have changed, and the deal has changed." Fat Tony was no longer smiling.

Fat Tony wasn't a boss in the Genovese Family at the time, but he was on his way up. His bosses had put him in charge of the numbers racket, and I guess he wanted to flex his muscles for Bumpy. But more intimidating than his soft fat muscles were the lean ones possessed by "Trigger Mike" Coppola, a well-known mob assassin who was sitting next to Fat Tony.

But Bumpy refused to be intimidated. He gave a little laugh and stood up, and his men stood up alongside him. "I guess this meeting is over." He looked over at Joey A. "You need to get word to our friend about what is going on, and that I'm not too happy about it."

Joey A. looked at Bumpy and said quietly. "You trying to give me orders, Bumpy?"

Nat stepped forward but Bumpy pushed him back and said, "No. I wouldn't presume to give you orders, just as you know I won't be taking orders. As far as I'm concerned we're equals like we've always been. But I am requesting that when you next make contact with our friend you give him my best regards and let him know I was very happy to be of assistance while we were away together."

Joey A. nodded but said nothing else.

Bumpy and his men left, and headed for a storefront he'd rented with some of the money he'd gotten from Johnny Walker and the others. He got word to Ritchie Williams, Georgie Rose, Finley, Six-n-Eight, and Obadiah and told them to get there on the double. When they arrived he told them about the meeting.

"So what you gonna do now, Bumpy?" Steve Mitchell asked. "We going back to war?"

"Maybe. I don't know yet," Bumpy said. "I gotta figure out our next move." He noticed Six-n-Eight rubbing his hands together in a nervous fashion. "What's the matter with you? You turn yaller all of a sudden?"

"Bumpy, man, you know I'm doing business with the Italians now. Got my own little numbers spot, they throw a little loan sharking my way, and shit," Six-n-Eight replied, his eyes shifting around the room. "You know I ain't never gonna turn against you, but I'm not thinking I wanna be down making a move against them. And we ain't as young as we used to be."

The room grew silent. After a few minutes Bumpy turned to Nat. "I know you been working with the Italians since I been gone, too. You feel the same way as Six?"

"Fuck you for even asking, Bumpy," Nat said angrily. "I told you back in the day that youse my nigger and ain't shit change far as I'm concerned. I'll kill a guinea over you just as quick as I'd kill any other ofay. They ain't my brothers. You my brother. Tell me which one you want knocked off first and I'll go do it now."

"How do the rest of y'all feel about it?" Bumpy asked the other men in the room.

"I'm speaking for everyone but Six," Junie said. "We're all ready to go to the streets. Ain't no wop going to be running our thing."

Six-n-Eight sputtered, "Man, I didn't say –"

"We heard what you said, and what you didn't say," Nat challenged him. "Youse a no good mother—"

"Leave it alone, Nat," Bumpy waved him off. "Six, I know you well enough to know you ain't gonna move against us no matter who you in bed with. And I know you ain't gonna tell anybody anything you already heard. But you need to get the fuck up outta here now."

After Six-n-Eight left Nat looked at Bumpy and said, "What you think? We need to take care of Six?"

Bumpy shook his head. "He ain't no snitch, and he ain't no turncoat. He just ain't got no real loyalty. But we don't have to worry about him carrying shit back to the Italians on us. We known him too long to rub him out 'cause of something we *think* he might do. I don't go against my friends like that."

"So, okay, Bumpy. What's our first move?" Junie Byrd asked after things settled back down.

"I'm thinking we snatch a couple of them," Bumpy answered.

"What do you mean snatch?"

"Just like they snatched Casper Holstein back in the day that started the whole shit in the first place," Bumpy answered. "We return the favor. Get like a hunnert grand or so, double what they got for Casper, then turn them loose. That will let them know we mean business." "Yeah? And what you think gonna happen after that?" Finley asked. "Them motherfuckers gonna go after us with all they got."

"If they do, we go right back at them," Bumpy answered. "And we give them as good as we got."

Yes, I know this all sounds unbelievable, but I believed Bumpy when he told me. And then years after Bumpy died Ralph Salerno (no relation to Fat Tony), a police detective who was New York City's expert on organized crime, said in an interview that he heard the whole conversation on tape because the police department had already put a bug in the storefront. He said that when he heard the tape he had to replay it twice because he couldn't believe what he was hearing – a gang of black men talking about kidnapping members of the Mafia. But that was Bumpy.

It never did come to that, because Joey A. did actually let Lucky Luciano know what was going on, and even though Lucky was now in exile in Naples, Italy he sent word back that when it came to Bumpy the mob had to not only honor the deal he'd struck with Bumpy, but to give him anything he wants.

It seems that when Bumpy was sent to Dannemora in 1938, Lucky Luciano was already there. The two men were already friendly, if not friends, and they became closer while in the joint. Especially after a man tried to shank Lucky in the prison yard and Bumpy pushed Luciano out of the way and slugged the guy.

"Why didn't you tell me what you did for our friend?" Joey A. asked when he turned over the keys to Bumpy's brand new 1948 black Cadillac.

"It wasn't for me to tell," Bumpy answered simply.

Bumpy still didn't like Joey A., but he gave the man credit – if Joey A. had ignored his request and not gotten word back to Lucky about what was going on, a whole new war would have broken out in Harlem. He realized Joey A. probably didn't like him anymore than he liked Joey A., but the man did the right thing by making sure Lucky knew what was going on.

Bumpy's relationship with the East Side Italians were sometimes rocky, once he got out of Dannemora, but he never backed down. He was determined that they deal with him before they tried to step to anyone in Harlem, and when didn't, Bumpy made sure there was Hell to pay.

"I can remember one time I was at Harris's Bar on the corner of 132nd Street and 7th Avenue, and two

Italian guys came and dragged one of the colored fellas out," William "Pop" Gates, the late basketball legend and NBA Hall of Famer, told me shortly after Bumpy's death. "There was a bunch of us in the bar when it happened, but there weren't one of us made a move to the help the guy because we knew that was the Mafia, and we weren't getting mixed up in that."

One of the men in the bar ran next door to Wells Restaurant, one of Bumpy's hang-outs to tell him what happened, and not finding him there, telephoned our house.

"Personally, I didn't see the sense in it because everyone knew if the Italians took someone for a ride he wasn't going to be seen alive again," said Pop, who was coaching the Harlem Globetrotters at the time. "But a few minutes later Bumpy came to the bar, and started asking people what went down."

After gathering as much information as he could, Bumpy jumped into his black Cadillac and sped away. Nat Pettigrew, Obadiah, Junie Byrd, and Steve Mitchell followed in another car. An hour later the formerly kidnapped man walked back in the bar, smiling and free.

"We were shocked. You have to understand, this was quite a remarkable feat," said Pop. "We all knew that Bumpy had connections with the Italians, but I don't think anyone thought he would be able to pull something like that off. I mean, that guy had messed up with the mob, and Bumpy was able to get him off. It was quite remarkable."

There was a bar on Lenox and 132nd Street called the Yellow Front, which was a hang out spot for Blacks, but the East Side Italians would sometimes go over there and hang out, too -- which was okay with Bumpy. What wasn't okay was when the place was crowded, and the Italians would tell everyone to get out so they could have seats. Bumpy would go over there and tell them to get "their asses up and out," and not come back to Harlem until they learned better manners than to take a seat from a lady.

Bumpy's relationship with the Italian mob was good in the thirties, but only cordial in the forties. He made it clear, if they wanted him to show respect, they had some respect they needed to be showing, too. "They're not coming down here to black Harlem and flex muscles and not expect us take off our shirts and show them what we got," he would say.

There's a lot of books written by so-called experts on the Italian Mafia that says Bumpy was their henchman, and worked for the Italian mob. Nothing could be further from the truth. He worked with them sometimes, but never for them. But that's why we need more black people writing books to tell the real history. I'm glad, at 93, to do my part.

So Bumpy opened his numbers bank on 135th Street along with Hoss Steele, of all people. I guess he figured as long as he kept his eye on Hoss he'd make a great partner because weren't no runner or player gonna try and beat them outta no number with Hoss watching the books – because no one could keep track of money the way Hoss could, except maybe ole penny pinching Finley.

Anyway, they opened the spot in February 1948, and I met him that April.

Life as Bumpy's girlfriend was dizzying and glorious. Even though neither of us drank, we were out at theaters, clubs, and gambling joints almost every night and he introduced me to a whole bunch of celebrities I'm positive I would never have met had it not been for him. I was in awe when he introduced me to Bill "Bojangles" Robinson, the famous tap dancer and movie star. Bojangles lived in Sugar Hill, and I'd

seen him around town, but never had the nerve to say
anything to him. Still, I knew the rumors about him
being a hard drinking and hard gambling man. Yes, I
said hard drinking, and I'm well aware of all the
biographies that said Bojangles didn't drink. The
biographers lied, or Bojangles lied to them, I don't
know. Bumpy and his friends used to say that white
folks just didn't know how great an actor Bojangles
really was because he sure fooled the Hell out of them
with his big grin and ingratiating manner. In reality
Bojangles could be evil as hell, and had a terrible
temper – especially when he drank. I saw that for
myself one night when I went with Bumpy to a Georgia
Skin game at the Theresa Hotel. Skin was Bojangles'
favorite card game just like it was Bumpy's. It was
about 4:30 a.m., and Bojangles was by this time drunk,
and mad because he'd lost all of his money.

"I know y'all niggers been cheating me," a
drunken Bojangles said. "And I'ma kill all y'all
motherfuckers up in here right now if you don't give
me back my money."

Then he pulled out a pearl-handled gun and shot
a couple of bullets into the ceiling. Most of the
gamblers just sighed and gave him his money back –
they knew when they sat down what Bojangles was
capable of, but they always let him sit in because his
presence brought in easy marks for them to prey on.
Bumpy just laughed, but then when Bojangles turned
and pointed the gun at him he looked the older man
straight in the eye and said, "I know you drunk, man,
but I also know you ain't that damn drunk." Bojangles
grinned and put the gun back in his pocket. "Yeah,
okay, Bumpy."

Finley was another one who'd never give
Bojangles back his money. I think Finley would take a

bullet before handing anyone any money. He was just like that.

Bumpy also introduced me to Sugar Ray Robinson and his wife, Edna Mae who used to be a Cotton Club dancer. Edna Mae was a pretty woman, and in fact she was on the very first cover of Jet Magazine. Edna was a pleasant enough woman at times, but at other times she was hard to be around because she was always showing off. She was *so* very materialistic. I remembered one time she was boasting to me about a beautiful mink coat Sugar Ray had bought her, and talking about the fact that it cost him $10,000. I just looked at her, and then made a big deal of looking at my watch, which was solid gold, weighed almost a 1/2 pound, and was covered with diamonds and rubies. Edna eyes widened, but she couldn't bring herself to ask me about it, so I had to help her out.

"Isn't it nice?" I said in my most friendly best girlfriend voice. "And you're not going to believe it, but Bumpy paid just as much for this little bitty watch as your husband paid for that great big coat of yours. Isn't that something?"

Hmph! Wasn't no woman going to out materialistic me.

Bumpy and Sugar Ray were very good friends, and he used to take me to all of his fights, as well as any of the other big prize fights going on at the time. But there was one fight that will always stand out in my mind. It was a night I'd never forget, but not because of what happened in the boxing ring, but what happened after the fight.

It was September 1948, a few months after Bumpy and I met, and shortly before we were married. Tony Zale, the world middleweight champion was defending his crown for the first time since winning it back from Rocky Graziano. His opponent was some

Mayme Johnson
and Karen E. Quinones Miller

French guy, and the match was being held across the bridge in New Jersey.

Bumpy got us tickets and we drove up to New Jersey that evening, and Six-n-Eight and his girlfriend rode in the backseat of our car. Junie Byrd and his wife, Mattie; Nat and his girlfriend Frances, John Levy and his girl, Peggy Sharpe; and Georgie Rose and his latest, also went – but they took their own automobiles.

On the way Six-n-Eight told us that the Italians he worked for gave him two thousand dollars to lay a bet on the Frenchman, but they had to be crazy because Zale was going to cream the guy.

"Don't you think Zale's gonna whup him?" Six-n-Eight asked Bumpy.

Bumpy nodded and said, "Man, I put my money on Zale. Them Italians must be nuts."

"Yeah, that's just what I figure," Six-n-Eight said, "but I ain't complaining. Because I took their money and put it on Zale. When he wins I get to keep the money and they won't never know." Then he started laughing.

Well, Bumpy near drove off the road. "What?" he shouted at Six-n-Eight when he pulled over. "Man, don't be fucking with those people's money!"

But Six-n-Eight just waved him off and said he knew what he was doing. Me and his girlfriend just shrugged our shoulders. We couldn't care less about the bet or anything. We just wanted to hurry up and get to the fight so we could show off our clothes.

Well, wouldn't you know that after 11 rounds, Zale – who was known as the "Man of Steel" and who had just beaten boxer Rocky Graziano in two out of three legendary matches – wouldn't come out to fight in the 12th round, saying he'd had enough? All of a sudden Cerdan was the new world middleweight champion and Six-n-Eight looked like he was about to die.

142

That was Zale's last fight, he retired after that. And Cerdan lost the championship, in his very next fight, to Jake LaMotta – aka The Raging Bull. Later it came out that LaMotta had thrown his fight with Billy Fox in order to get that title shot with Cerdan. He said he was ordered to do so by the Mafia so they could make a mint on the betting line. Now, if that's a lie it's Mr. LaMotta who told it. So who knows? Maybe the Italians weren't so crazy putting all that money on Cerdan, after all. There's no doubt that Six-n-Eight was crazy not to have just followed orders.

"Where you going to head now?" Bumpy asked Six-n-Eight when we got out the stadium.

"What do you mean? I'm heading home."

Bumpy and them looked at him like he was crazy. "Man, you'd better haul your ass out of New York after messing up those people's money."

Six-n-Eight wouldn't listen, though. He said he'd talk to them and explain what happened, and give them the two thousand out of his numbers spot.

"Are you crazy?" Bumpy started laughing. "They gonna want a helluva lot more than two thousand. They're going to want the money they woulda made on the fight if you'd done what the hell you was supposed to do, and they're going to smoke you if they don't get it."

"I told you before, I'm tight with the Italians," Six-n-Eight said. "Just leave it to me. I can handle myself."

About a week later Six-n-Eight lay dying on the sidewalk in front of his mother's building on 150th Street, his body filled with bullets.

I think, in fact, I know, that's when it hit me what kind of lives Bumpy and his friends lived – and I wondered what the hell it was I was getting into. Yeah, Bumpy was the top man in his crew, but even the top man had enemies. What the hell was I doing with someone who could be shot and killed at any moment?

Three weeks later Bumpy and I got married.

Chapter Eight – Dark Betrayal

We moved into a beautiful 3-bedroom apartment on the corner of 120th Street and Fifth Avenue, right across the street from Mount Morris Park (they call it Marcus Garvey Park now, I think.) It was me and Bumpy in one bedroom; my daughter, Ruthie, in one bedroom; and Bumpy's daughter, Elease, in another.

Bumpy's sister, Genevieve, had been taking care of Elease while he was away at Dannemora, but now that we were married, and he actually had a settled home, he took over custody. Elease was 15, the same age as Ruthie, and she was quite a handful. Genevieve had complained to Bumpy that the girl was sneaking out meeting grown men and running the streets, so Bumpy knew that she was going to need some serious supervision. That was delegated to me. And Lord knows I did the best I could, but that girl was something else. She had some serious issues, but then how could you blame her? Here she was her mother dead, her father in prison, and having to be raised by an aunt. And I know Genevieve – she wasn't the most loving person in the world – and I'm sure she threw up in that girls face that her mother was a whore and her daddy a jailbird. Genevieve was just like that. I'm sure I would have had issues if I had to hear that from the time I was two until the time I was 15. Wouldn't you?

Bumpy and I had been married only two months before he met Flash Walker.

Flash Walker. How I hate that name.

I hate that man more than I've hated anyone before I met him in 1948, or anyone I've met since. It's because of him that Bumpy was convicted of drug conspiracy and had to do time at Alcatraz. It's because of him that Bumpy was taken away from me after only six years into our marriage.

William "Pop" Gates was the one who introduced them. Pop was a real likeable young man who had a lot going for him. He was a star with the Harlem Rennies, the premiere black basketball team at the time, and he would later become coach of the legendary Harlem Globetrotters, and in 1989 was inducted into the National Basketball League's Hall of Fame. He would have been a star in the NBA, but by the time they started letting black players into the league in 1950 Pop was already 33 years old – over the hill for a basketball player the NBA owners thought.

Pop first met Bumpy when the boy was only 15-years-old and attending Benjamin Franklin High School in East Harlem in 1932, the year Bumpy got out of Sing Sing and started his infamous feud with Dutch Schultz. He approached Bumpy about a job collecting numbers, but after Bumpy found out he was a high school basketball star he refused to let Pop work the numbers game, but threw money at him whenever he heard Pop was in need. Pop never forgot, and was always one of Bumpy's biggest supporters later in life. Pop was a real stand-up guy, and it really ate him up when he realized that an introduction he made would bring about Bumpy's downfall.

Back then NBA players were making like $4,000 a year. Players for the black basketball teams were making a mere fraction of that, maybe five or six hundred a year, so they usually had a part-time hustle. One of Pop's hustles was managing smalltime boxers.

It was in December of 1948, and I was with Bumpy at Lump's Restaurant on 134th Street and Seventh Avenue when Pop came over to our table.

"So, Bumpy I hear you're back in action. You got any openings in any of your spots?" Pop asked after greeting us and taking a seat.

Bumpy looked at him and just laughed. "Man, I told you years ago I ain't letting you in the rackets. Get the hell away from me."

Pop laughed with him for a minute then explained he wasn't asking for himself, but for a young boxer he was managing.

"He's a nice guy, and got the gift of gab. He's a damn good boxer, too, but he got a glass jaw. I can't do nothing for him, but he's a real cool cat so I was hoping you might be able to throw something his way."

Bumpy just shook his head and said he was just getting his operation back together, but he already had all the workers he needed.

"You don't have nothing? Bumpy, he's a really cool cat," Pop pleaded. "He just needs a break. Can't you find something for him?"

"Naw, man. Like I said, I already got all my spots covered," Bumpy said.

"Well," then Pop looked at me. "What about around your house? You don't want your pretty lady to be washing windows and hauling trash, do you?"

"I can take care of my own household, thank you very much," I said primly.

"I wasn't trying to insult you, Miss Mayme," Pop said hurriedly. "I just want to see if I can get Flash some kind of work. The boy doesn't even have a dime to buy food. Makes a dollar a week cleaning up the poolroom. The kid's running around in sneakers with holes in them even now with snow on the ground."

I have to admit, I was feeling a little sorry for this Flash guy even though I'd never met him, and I could see Bumpy was relenting too, so I said, "Well, I don't know. Maybe I can use a little help from time to time."

Bumpy just shrugged and said, "Yeah, well send him over to my spot on 135th Street tomorrow and I'll look him over."

Late the next afternoon Bumpy came home and had Flash in tow. He was a good-looking young man, dark-skinned, with deep-set eyes and a smile that seemed a permanent part of his face. And charming. Charming as hell. Flash had a way of charming everyone around him, and I could see that Bumpy was already taken by the young man. See, Bumpy never had a son, and Flash, I guess at the time, was about 19 or 20 years old. And Flash was a talker. Ooh, he could talk. He complimented the furnishing, complimented Bumpy on all the books in the library, complimented our artwork – he just had a comment and a compliment about everything; and didn't seem like a phony word was coming out of his mouth. You could tell he was really impressed, and even a little in awe. Then he inhaled and said, "Umph! Is that collard greens I smell cooking in your kitchen, Miss Mayme? Them's the best smelling collards I ever had the pleasure of smelling." I was flattered, of course, and I had made up my mind that as soon as Bumpy left I was going to fix Flash a big plate of greens, chicken and corn bread. But to my surprise, Bumpy beat me to the punch.

"Mayme," he said, "why don't you go ahead and fix the boy a plate. Looks like he could use some food."

And he sure did look like it. The boy was skinny as a rail, and the raggedy clothes he was wearing was just hanging off of him. I fixed both him and Bumpy a big heaping portion of food and set it on the table, and I've never seen anyone devour a plate of food as fast as that boy did that day. He was finished before Bumpy even had taken two bites of his own food. Bumpy laughed and told me to fix him another plate, and I did. And this time around Flash took his time, and complimented me every time he took a forkful. I admit Flash really won me over. Every cook likes to be complimented and Flash was laying it on so thick I almost blushed. Bumpy didn't say much as Flash was talking, but I could see he really liked Flash, too.

Flash started working around the house the next day, washing windows, scrubbing the floors, hauling trash and running errands. He was always respectful to me and to Elease and Ruthie, and soon he became like part of the family – and you could see Bumpy's fondness for him growing. He started treating Flash like he was a son. Treated him better than a son. Bumpy really loved Flash, and Flash loved Bumpy, too. I think maybe Elease and Ruthie were a little jealous of the relationship he was developing with Bumpy, although they didn't say anything at the time.

But Flash kept begging Bumpy to put him down at one of his number spots. I don't know why Bumpy was so hesitant, but finally after a week or so he gave him a chance. Bumpy came home that night and told me that Flash was one of the best number runners he'd ever seen. Said that he gave him a short route – one where usually only one or two hundred dollars were collected from people wanting to play the numbers -- but somehow Flash brought in five hundred dollars.

"It can't be that he included his own money in to impress me because he don't have dough like that," Bumpy said. "I'm going with him tomorrow and see what the hell it is he's doing."

Well, Bumpy would later tell me, Flash just charmed people into putting more money on a number than they intended. If for instance a woman told him she wanted a dime on 125 he'd say something like,

"125, huh? Oh yeah, that's a good one. Heck, I think I might put a dollar on it myself, I could use the six hundred dollars. Let's see, you say you want a dime on it? That'll get you sixty dollars. Come on, now, Miss Lady. You going to tell me that you can't use more than sixty dollars? Put another nickel on it so you can buy yourself one of them pretty dresses from up on the Avenue and show off that gorgeous shape of yours."

Or if someone told them that they dreamt about a cemetery and wanted to play 953 because Madame Fu-Fu's Lucky Dream Book listed that number for cemeteries, Flash would whip out the book (seems he carried a few of the different dream books around) and look up cemeteries and say something like, "Well, you might wanna put a little something on 864 and 851, cause depending on what you was doing in the cemetery it might be one of those numbers. Ain't no harm in hedging your bets."

And damn if they didn't do just what he suggested, Bumpy said.

Flash was a real hustler, there was no doubt, and soon he was raking in more money than any of Bumpy's other workers. I lost him as a helper around the house, but I was still seeing him on the regular because Bumpy was always having him over for dinner.

Then one morning Flash stopped by and he was coughing up a storm. Seemed like he was coughing so hard he was going to cough up a lung. I tried to make him sit down and drink some tea and eat some chicken soup, but he was coughing so hard he couldn't keep anything down. Bumpy stopped in a few minutes later and I told him that he needed to get Flash to see a doctor and quick.

Bumpy said, "Aw, he'll be fine, Mayme. You worry too much." Just then Flash had one of his coughing fits and actually coughed up some blood.

Bumpy didn't waste any time. He damn near carried Flash out to the car and drove him to Harlem Hospital. Dr. Louise Carter was working there, and she took care of Flash; had him admitted that same day.

Now this was back in 1948, mind you, and tuberculosis was still raging in New York because they didn't have the TB vaccine then. Everyone was scared that Flash might have TB, and that was real contagious. They put him in isolation and ran all kinds of tests on him. Turns out he didn't have TB, just pneumonia. And that's because he was walking around in the middle of winter with snow on the ground with just sneakers and a thin coat. And that's when Bumpy found out that Flash didn't have any place to stay. He was actually sleeping on a pool table at the local pool hall down the street.

Well, when Flash heard he didn't have TB he signed himself out the hospital and, wearing nothing but a bathrobe and them old raggedy sneakers, he walked the 15 blocks from Harlem Hospital back to our place on 120th Street. When he rung the bell I opened the door and he 'bout fell into my arms. Bumpy was home, and he tried to carry Flash back up to the hospital but Flash fought him on it. Then Flash said something that made me cry, and Bumpy fight back tears. Flash told us that he'd been an orphan, that his mother abandoned him on a doorstep when he was an infant, and that he'd been shuffled around from foster home to foster home all of his childhood. Said that even when he was grown, he never seemed to catch a lucky break – never finding a job which he enjoyed or in which he excelled, and constantly being picked up by the police for vagrancy or disorderly conduct charges. The two weeks that he'd known Bumpy were the best two weeks in his life, he'd never felt more needed and loved. And, he said, he wasn't going to blow all of it because of some stupid cold.

Well, that was that. We had a three bedroom apartment, Bumpy and I had the front room, we moved Ruthie into the back room with Elease, and we set Flash up in the middle room so I could nurse him back to good health. When Flash got back on his feet after a couple of weeks, Bumpy took him shopping, and bought him a whole wardrobe of fine clothes. Flash wound up staying with us for six months in that little room, and he was as happy as a bug in a rug.

It was kind of cute the way Flash looked up to Bumpy. He got to where he started walking like him, talking like him, and even switched his brand of cigarettes to Pall Mall, which was Bumpy's brand. Actually, now that I think about it, I'm not sure Flash smoked at all before he met Bumpy.

Flash even took to bringing girls he was dating around so he could get me and Bumpy's approval. And oh, he had a lot of girls. Flash was a good looking man even before he was wearing nice clothes, and now that he was dressing sharp he was pulling girls like crazy. Bumpy got a kick out of it, because Bumpy was a ladies man himself, but he couldn't hold a candle to Flash. That man could talk the panties off a nun.

In just a matter of time Bumpy started taking Flash around on his business runs. Those were the little short trips Bumpy had to take from time-to-time to get someone who stepped out of line back in line, if you know what I mean. Pop was right, Flash was good with his hands, and none of the guys he had to work over with Bumpy ever swung at his jaw, so he was very effective. Bumpy was a fighter, and always admired a good fighter. Him and Flash grew tighter and tighter.

Both of them loved to gamble – Bumpy's game, of course, was still Georgia Skin, but he would lay a bet down on anything. And Flash was a pool shark to his heart. They would go into a pool hall and Bumpy would stake Flash against the best players in the joint, and then the two would split the winnings. Bumpy would come home after a big night of winnings, shake his head and say, "I ain't never seen anyone put English on a ball like Flash."

Soon he was taking Flash along with him to meetings even with the Italians, something I'd very rarely seen him do with anyone else. But he really trusted Flash, and it never hurt to have someone you trusted along with you to watch your back. And Flash would step to someone in a minute if he thought they disrespected Bumpy, whether Bumpy was around or not. Flash's temper was just like his name, quick and fierce; something else he shared with Bumpy. He would beat someone down in a minute if he thought they were disrespecting his new father.

Now, let's stop for a minute. I know you've never heard of Flash Walker before, but I think you may find some of the elements of this story sound familiar. That's because Frank Lucas, the dope dealer depicted by Denzel Washington in the movie *American Gangster*, pretty much took Flash Walker's relationship with Bumpy and claimed it as his own.

Frank said in the article "The Return of Super Fly," which was printed in New York Magazine in 2000, that he met Bumpy at a pool hall in 1948, and that Bumpy staked him for $1,000 against some make-believe guy named Ice Pick Red. He also said that Bumpy took him shopping for clothes, and that he stayed with Bumpy and me in our apartment on 121st Street (we actually lived on 120th Street, but Frank didn't know because he didn't know Bumpy back then and never set foot in that apartment!). He then went on to say that he was Bumpy's bodyguard and enforcer,

153

and accompanied Bumpy to meetings with the Italian
mob.

Met Bumpy in 1948 . . . pool shark . . . new
wardrobe . . . stayed with us for six months . . . acted as
bodyguard and enforcer . . .treated like a son – this was
Flash Walker's life. Frank Lucas just co-opted it
because he thought he could get away with it since
there aren't many people alive who remember Flash. I
remember Flash. I remember the good times with Flash
and, God help me, I'll never forget the bad.

There were a lot of folks jealous of Flash's
relationship with Bumpy, and they looked for ways to
tear Flash down, and Flash gave them plenty of
ammunition. He was charming, but the closer he
became to Bumpy the more arrogant he became. He
went around bragging to people about how tight he was
with Bumpy, and that if they messed with him they
were messing with Bumpy and vice-versa.

One day Flash walked into Wells Restaurant on
Seventh Avenue near 132nd Street, and ran into a beat
cop who had once busted him on a disorderly conduct
charge years before. The cop, Johnny Jenkins, was just
in there chatting with a friend, when Flash strolled over
to him and said, "Man, you ain't nothing but a punk.
Let me see you try and fuck with me now. I got
something for your ass."

The cop turned and was going to say something
to him, but the friend whom he'd been talking to said,
"Don't pay him no mind. He's just spouting off with
the mouth." Well, the police officer knew that Flash
was running with Bumpy, and he didn't want any
unnecessary trouble so he took his friend's advice and
tried to ignore Flash.

But Flash wouldn't let up. He walked over to
the bar and continued ragging the cop, talking about his
mother and saying all kinds of ridiculous things about

154

what he was going to do to him the next time he saw him. The officer finally stood up to leave, but he had to pass Flash to get to the door. Don't you know that fool actually took a drink and threw it in the cop's face? Well, the police officer had had enough. He grabbed Flash by the collar, threw him down on the bar, and started punching him in the face. Flash was a good fighter, and he managed to hold his own against the cop, but then the cop pulled out his gun and pointed it at Flash's chest. Just then Bumpy walks in and sees what's happening. He drew a pistol out of his pocket and put it to the cop's head but before he could pull the trigger Junie Byrd – who had been there the whole time – shouted for him to stop, and that Flash had instigated the fight. That's the only thing that saved that officer's life that day. Bumpy was ready to kill a police officer to protect his protégé!

None of Bumpy's old friends, like Junie, Steve, Nat and Finley, liked Flash all that much, but they tolerated him because of Bumpy's affection for the young man. After that incident, though, even they started telling Bumpy that he needed to cut Flash loose, because the man was going to cause more trouble than he was worth. Bumpy didn't listen, though. The man was naturally hard-headed, and even more so when it came to Flash. Bumpy and Flash stayed tight for almost two years, and Bumpy even allowed Flash to introduce himself as Bumpy's son.

Bumpy's bank was bringing in about $60,000 a month, not at all a shabby amount, but he was determined to increase it. While he was away at Dannemora the Italians had opened a bank in the same neighborhood, and even though they left him alone about his bank, they hadn't closed theirs, and so they were splitting customers between them. The regular payout on a number hit was 600-1, meaning if you put a dollar on a number you'd get paid $600. Of course the odds of you hitting the three numbers was 1000-1 so that's how the bank made their profit. What Bumpy decided to do, to get all of the customers in the neighborhood to play at his spot, was to increase their payout to 800-1 on Tuesdays, Wednesdays, Thursdays, Fridays and Saturdays, and on Monday he ran a special – a cool $1,000 payout for a one dollar hit, which meant the bank wouldn't make any profit at all. Well, within two weeks the Italians went ahead and shut down their spot, and Bumpy had the neighborhood all to himself again, and he eventually went back to the regular 600 to 1 payoff. But not before he and Hoss ran into a little trouble.

Dickie Carter was a nice kid from down the block, and Bumpy knew some of his family so when he asked Bumpy if he could run numbers for him, Bumpy agreed. He was about 20, right around Flash's age, and he turned out to be a pretty decent runner. But then one day, just as he was returning to the spot to turn in his numbers he ran into one of his regular customers. The guy was with some girl, and wanted to show off, so instead of putting his regular fifty cents on his number, he gave Dickie a ten dollar bill. Now here's where Dickie messed up. Instead of pulling out his number pad and writing down the number, he just wrote the number down on the ten the guy gave him and went on over to the spot and turned his numbers in. What a runner is supposed to do is let his controller, the guy running the spot, know which numbers were played heavy so the controller can try to lay some of the action off on another spot so if the number hit it won't break the bank. But when Dickie turned in his numbers he forgot about the number he'd written down on that ten dollar bill, even though he turned the ten in with the rest of the money he collected. And wouldn't you know the

156

number hit? And oh yeah, I forgot to mention this was on a Monday, while Bumpy was still running the $1,000 to 1 special.

The guy was at the spot bright and early the next morning to collect, and all hell broke loose. The controller showed him the pad that Dickie had turned in, and that it didn't have the guy putting a ten on the number, but the guy kept insisting. Then Dickie walked in like he didn't have a care in the world until he saw the guy at the spot and suddenly it all came back to him. He started apologizing, saying he was sorry, but that the guy wasn't lying. Well, now the controller remembered that when he counted Dickie's money up he was ten dollars over, but he'd just shrugged it off and showed it on the books as "extra," and sent it over with the rest of the day's receipts. But the controller wasn't letting on he remembered, because he didn't know how his bankers – Bumpy and Hoss – wanted to handle it.

The controller called Bumpy and told him what happened, and then Bumpy called Hoss and told him to meet him at our apartment on 120th Street, where they kept the receipts. They went through the money and sure enough they found the ten dollar bill with the number on it. They owed that man $10,000 fair and square, and their bank was going to be wiped out since they hadn't had the opportunity to lay any of the action off.

Hoss' solution? "Man, the only way that nigga is going to get $10,000 is at the point of my .35."

I was listening to all this, and I started feeling sorry for the poor guy. Not that I thought Hoss was really going to kill him. See, Hoss wasn't really a killer. Oh, he'd beat you up real bad over some money, don't get me wrong. Bad enough to even make you wish you were dead, but he wasn't really into killing anyone unless it was a life and death situation. He just didn't have the heart of a killer. Now, Nat, well, he was another story. He wouldn't hurt a fly unless provoked, but when he felt it was in his best interest to make someone disappear, they was disappeared. But you know, Nat was a fair guy, and he wouldn't have hurt a man over some money that was rightly owed to him. The guy better thank his lucky stars that Bumpy was a fair guy, too.

He pretty much emptied out the bank, and then borrowed some money from Johnny Walker and Chink Cunningham, all told coming up with about $8,500. Then he went to the guy and explained that he was short, but he'd pay him the rest the following week. Well, the guy was shocked, and so was everyone else. It hadn't taken but a minute for everyone in the neighborhood to hear what had happened and all the bets were that Bumpy and Hoss weren't going to pay. It enhanced Bumpy's reputation that he did the right thing, but Hoss still wasn't too happy. Now understand, Bumpy still wasn't too thrilled about Hoss either – not just because he didn't want to pay off the guy but also because of the whole money thing while Bumpy was in Dannemora. But Bumpy had this thing about his old friends – no matter what they did, and how mad he got at them he'd never lay a finger on them. And boy, sometimes he'd get really mad.

Like the time he, Nat, and Chappy were eating at Red Roosters, on Seventh Avenue, near 138th Street. Chappy was kidding Bumpy about something and Bumpy told him to lay off. Chappy just ignored him and kept on with the kidding. Bumpy warned him again, but Chappy just kept on going and just kept on going. Suddenly Bumpy got up from the table, walked into the kitchen and came back with an axe -- you know, one of those red axes they used to make restaurants keep around in case of fires. Chappy saw Bumpy coming toward the table with that axe and he 'bout peed in his pants. Nat said he couldn't believe it either.

"Bumpy, you okay, man?" Nat asked. But Bumpy didn't answer. Instead he walked past the table and out the door. Nat and Chappy looked at each for a moment, then rushed out of the Red Rooster's to see just what the hell Bumpy was up to. They got outside just in time to see Bumpy bring the axe down on the roof of Chappy's brand new 1949 white Cadillac.

"Bumpy, what you doing, man?" Chappy cried as he tried to pull Bumpy away from the car. But Bumpy ignored him and kept swinging the axe.

"Bumpy, please just go ahead and kill me, but leave my ride alone," Chappy pleaded, which made Nat start laughing.

"Spoken like a true pimp," he said.

But Bumpy just ignored both of them and he kept swinging that axe until the car was literally cut in half. Then he stopped, straightened up his clothes, returned the axe to the kitchen, walked back out the bar and got into his own car and drove off.

Nat thought the whole thing was hilarious, but Chappy wasn't all that amused. But you'd best believe that Chappy knew to lay off Bumpy the next time Bumpy told him to lay off.

But the thing was, as mad as Chappy had made him, Bumpy would never have taken a swing at him. Or Hoss. Or Finley. Or Junie Byrd. Or Wesley Goodwin. Or Obadiah. Or Steve Mitchell. Or Georgie Rose. Or Nat. Or Ritchie Williams. Or anyone who'd been with him from the beginning and stuck by him during the war with Dutch Schultz, when allying yourself with Bumpy meant you basically had a price on your head. Bumpy might go ahead and get mad at them, but he never ever stopped speaking to them, not even for a minute. That was Bumpy. He was loyal to his friends, and his friends were just as loyal to him. His real friends, anyway.

So even though he and Hoss weren't exactly thrilled with each other, they still had each other's back, even when Hoss decided to pull out of the bank and leave Bumpy on his own. To Hoss' credit, he did wait until all of the money had been paid to the guy.

Bottom line was Bumpy kept the bank and Hoss just went back to concentrating on his loan sharking business fulltime. And so then here comes more trouble.

Red Dillard, that old handsome devil, needed to borrow a quick five hundred bucks, and so like every other sporting man in Harlem needing a loan he looks up Hoss Steele. The deal was Red Dillard was supposed to pay the money back in two weeks along with whatever the interest was. Now, five hundred bucks, even with interest, was nothing, and Red Dillard should have had no problem paying the loan off. But the thing was Red Dillard didn't like paying back money. Hoss knew that when he loaned Red Dillard the money, but I guess he thought that Red Dillard wouldn't cross him. I don't know why he thought that, though. Well, when the two weeks came and went and Red Dillard didn't show with the money Hoss went looking for him. He found him at Shep's Bar and Grill on 145th Street. 8th Avenue. The two men passed a few words, and then Hoss – true to form – took a swing at Red Dillard. I did mention earlier that Red Dillard was one tough customer himself, right? Well, the two started brawling, but after about ten minutes Red Dillard pulls a gun out of his pocket and starts shooting at Hoss. Altogether he fired three shots, and one shot actually grazed Hoss' head. Discretion being the better part of valor, Hoss scrammed, but Red Dillard was arrested on a gun charge when a cop who heard the shooting ran into Shep's.

Red Dillard was let out on $3,500 bail, and a few days later a bandaged Hoss saw him at Harris' Bar. Bumpy was there, and so was Wesley Goodwin, Junie Byrd, Nat Pettigrew and Steve Mitchell.

"Man, if I had a gun I'd shoot that pretty-ass nigger right now," Hoss grumbled to his friends.

Bumpy nodded, took another sip of his ginger ale, and said, "No problem." He reached into his pocket and passed Hoss a .38.

"Go for it," Steve Mitchell said.

So Hoss walks over to the end of the bar where Red Dillard is standing and points the gun at him. "You owe me some money and I want it right now," Hoss said.

"I thought he just said he was going to shoot him. What's he talking to him for?" Nat asked.

"Hell if I know," Bumpy answered.

Meanwhile, Red seems unfazed by Hoss and the .38.

"Man, I ain't giving you shit," he said with a sneer.

"Oh you going to give me my money, nigger. Or I'm going to shoot your ass."

Red shrugged and said, "Yeah? Well, go ahead and shoot." Then he turned back to his drink.

Steve Mitchell yelled, "Man, Hoss. What you doing? Go ahead and shoot his ass."

Nat said, "Ain't this a damn shame? Got the gun. Got it pointed at him. And he's too scared to shoot. What kind of shit is that?"

"I ain't scared," Hoss shouted at him. When I found out about all this later, I truly did believe that Hoss was telling the truth, I don't think he was scared.

But see, like I said earlier, Hoss wasn't a cold-blooded killer like some folks. If Bumpy hadn't given him that gun he probably woulda went over there and beat the crap out of Red. And remember, Hoss had his share of shootouts during the Dutch Schultz war, but in those instances he was shooting at people who were shooting at him. This was different.

"Well, if you ain't scared go ahead and shoot that nigger," Steve Mitchell said.

"Yeah, punk motherfucker," Red said with a laugh. "Go ahead and shoot."

Bumpy slammed his fist down on the bar. "Will you listen to this shit?" he demanded. "The man welshed on his loan, took a shot at you, and now he's calling you a punk motherfucker and you there holding a gun and ain't pulling the damn trigger?" He jumped up from the stool and started walking over to the end of the bar where Hoss and Red were. "Give me my gun. I'll shoot the nigger."

Nat and Steve Mitchell just laughed, but before Hoss could turn over the gun Wesley Goodwin and Junie Byrd pushed him away from Bumpy.

"Bumpy, this ain't your fight, man," Wesley Goodwin said.

"Fuck that. He's fucking with my man."

Junie, always the voice of reason, stepped in close to Bumpy and said quiet enough for only Bumpy to hear. "Man, it ain't like Hoss is dead or in the hospital and can't take care of his shit himself. You handle this for him now and he's not going to be able to hold his head up in the streets."

Bumpy hesitated. "Yeah, you're right. But someone needs to teach this punk a lesson, though." He looked over where Red had been sitting, but the man was gone.

"Damn." Bumpy said, then turned to look at Hoss. "What? You turn punk all of a sudden?"

"I ain't no punk, man," Hoss protested. "I tried to shoot but the gun misfired. Y'all didn't see me pull the trigger?"

"Get the fuck outta here, man," Nat said with a laugh.

"Fuck it. It's over," Bumpy said. "Drinks are on me."

Red did finally pay Hoss, so things were cordial between them again, but it didn't take long for trouble to start up again, and it was because of Red Dillard again. And this time the trouble was big.

It was on a Saturday night in October of the same year, 1949. Gerald "Chink" Cunningham was at Covan's Playground, a bar & grill at 343 West 123rd street when Red Dillard Morrison and Louis "Fess" Taylor walked in the place. As Red was passing the bar, he "brushed" up against a young woman to whom Chink was talking. The woman said something about it, and Red told her to shut up, which prompted Chink to speak up in defense of the woman. Now, even though Chink was thoroughly in love with his wife, Evelyn, he was still a ladies man, just like Bumpy, but I never did get the impression that he and the girl was anything more than friends. But even just being friends, Chink was obligated to say something. So he said something to Red Dillard, and the two started arguing. Finally Chink, who was never much for violence and fighting, just said forget it, and walked outside to leave. Well, Red and Fess followed him out and words started flying back and forth again. Then Red takes out a knife and stabs Chink in the chest – puncturing his lung – and then slashes his throat for good measure.

Everyone was in shock – Chink was the last person anyone would ever think would get caught in some mess with Red, or anyone else for that matter, because Chink was just so easygoing and went out of his way to avoid trouble.

Fess managed to get away, but there must have been a cop in the area, because before Red could make his escape he was collared and thrown into the back seat of a police car, and taken to St. Luke's Hospital; not because he was hurt, but because the cop car was also transporting Chink rather than waiting on an ambulance.

It was Steve Mitchell who called Bumpy and told him what happened. We were in bed but Bumpy jumped up and threw on some clothes and sped over to the hospital – Steve had told him that they were saying they didn't think Chink was going to make it. Bumpy said he walked in the hospital and the first person he saw was Red Dillard in the lobby sitting around joking around with some nurses, and he just lost it. He jumped on the man, and would have killed him if six police officers hadn't pulled him off. They arrested Bumpy on the spot. Both Bumpy and Red Dillard made bail the following Monday – Bumpy getting out a few hours before Red.

When Red got out that afternoon he and Fess strolled into the lobby of the Hotel Theresa like they were the big men on campus, to their surprise all of the people hanging around the lobby scattered like roaches as soon as they saw them. They soon found out why. Two Cadillacs loaded with Bumpy and his crew -- Nat, Junie, Flash, Steve Mitchell, Obadiah, and Georgie Rose -- squealed to a stop in front of the hotel and Red and Fess just had time to make a quick escape through the back door of the hotel.

The next day, Tuesday, Red and Hoss Cartwright showed up at Harris's Bar – guns in hand – and Red said that he heard Bumpy was looking for him.

Bumpy pulled his gun, and the duo started shooting at each other. At first it was just the two of them, but then Hoss Cartwright started shooting at Bumpy, so Hoss Steele – bless his soul – pulled out a gun and a bonafide shootout began, finally spilling out into the street on Seventh Avenue. Somehow, no one was hurt, but it wasn't for lack of trying. Bumpy swore he was going to make Red pay for what he'd done to Chink. For his part, Red put the word out that he wasn't afraid of Bumpy and if the man wanted a war that he was ready to go to war. Like I said, Red was no punk.

A couple of days later Red saw Bumpy as Bumpy was coming out of one of his spots on 114th Street and Lenox Avenue, and took a shot at him. He would have got him, too, but just at the moment someone from inside the spot saw Red and yelled out to warn Bumpy. Bumpy ducked behind a parked car just in time, then he pulled his own gun and another shootout started, though this only lasted a couple of shots because the cops were on the scene in what seemed like seconds, and both Bumpy and Red jumped in their cars and sped off – in separate directions.

Since Bumpy had beat up on Red in front of the police that night in the hospital, Red didn't have to press charges against Bumpy, the state brought up the charges – but Red let it be known on the street that he did plan to testify that it was, indeed, Bumpy who assaulted him. Let me say right now it wasn't a snitch move – Red may have been a lot of things, but he wasn't a rat. The reason he was doing it was to let people know that he wasn't going to be intimidated into not testifying against Bumpy. And, for the record, once the trial rolled around Red got on the witness stand in December 1949 and said that Bumpy had nothing to do with the assault.

Red didn't like Bumpy, and Bumpy didn't like Red, but the two of them would later admit that they did truly admire each other. But I'm sure one of them would have eventually killed the other if Red hadn't gotten busted on a cocaine charge in early 1950. When he was sent away newspapers reported that thirty beautiful women were there to see him off, including Carrolle Drake Faulkner. Faulkner "a beautiful model type" was one of Red's many girls, and had managed to get thousands of dollars in cash and gifts out of the very married Heavyweight Champion, Joe Louis – all of which she promptly turned over to Red Dillard. Even the assistant district attorneys shook their heads when they saw Faulkner and the rest of Red's girls, and were heard to mutter that "he was one lucky nigger." Lucky, I don't know. But he sure was pretty.

1949 had been a helluva year for Bumpy; with the death of his good friend Dickie Wells due to a heart attack, along with Bub Hewlett, and Bill "Bojangles" Robinson and then the near death of Chink. Chink finally got out of the hospital shortly after 1950 rolled in, but then in October, all hell broke loose.

A pimp whom Flash had met during one of many short stints at Riker's Island ran into him on Seventh Avenue one afternoon, and the two started catching up on each other's lives. The pimp told Flash that he had run into a sweet deal, but was trying to figure out a way to cash in. It seems that the pimp had been getting big time cash from a white socialite, the daughter of a prominent politician. When the family found out they made her cut him loose, but not before he lifted her checkbook from her purse. The chick was so loaded with money, and so irresponsible, he was sure she didn't even miss the stolen checks, the pimp told Flash. All he needed was a way to cash the checks

166

without actually having to go to the bank and arousing suspicion.

Flash immediately saw a way for him to make a quick buck outside the money he making with Bumpy. He told his old friend that all he had to do was make the checks out to cash, and he would take the money from one of Bumpy's spots that he managed, and put the checks into Bumpy's bank account. Since the white chick had more money than the law allowed, and she didn't know the checks were missing, she'd never contact the bank to let them know the checks were fraudulent. The deal was sealed over a shot of whiskey and a round of pool.

Everything was smooth at first, Flash insisted that the checks never amount to more than one or two hundred dollars – a miniscule amount considering the money the pimp knew was in the white socialite's account. But after awhile the pimp and Flash became greedy, and were cashing in checks for seven and eight hundred dollars at a time.

It was four months into the scheme that Bumpy got a call from the Manufacturers Hanover Bank at 116th and Madison Avenue, asking him to come in and discuss his account. When he arrived, the bank president took him into a private office where he was introduced to the girl's father. The man accused Bumpy of stealing from his daughter, and threatened to turn him over to the police. Bumpy didn't know anything about the transactions, but he quickly figured out what was going on. He told the politician that if he went to the police the newspapers would get involved, and that would be bad for both of their careers, but assured the man that there would be no more checks cashed against his daughter's account.

Bumpy was furious, and was on his way to confront Flash at the spot he managed at the Theresa

Hotel on 125th Street, but stopped home first. While there he told me what happened. I'd seen Bumpy mad at Flash before, but never this mad, he was pacing back and forth across the room and ranting and raving about how Flash could have gotten him in serious trouble. Still, I figured he'd tell Flash off, put him on suspension for a few weeks and dock his pay for a few more, and then the whole thing would blow over.

But my daughter Ruthie, and Bumpy's daughter Elease – both now 16 and as shapely as grown women -- were in the next room, and they heard the whole thing. Suddenly Ruthie came in the living room and said, "Bumpy, I'm glad you're here. I wanted to tell you that when Flash was here earlier today he patted me on the butt."

Bumpy stopped in his tracks, and his mouth fell open. "He did what?" he finally said slowly and in a low voice.

I jumped up. "Ruthie, I've been home all day. How come you didn't say anything to me," I asked her.

"Because I wanted to tell Bumpy myself," she said nervously. I looked at her suspiciously. I had always suspected her of being jealous of Bumpy's relationship with Flash, but I didn't think she would stoop to lying on the man to break them up. Still, I couldn't be sure. I turned to Bumpy to try and calm him down, but his face had already turned a deep purple, and he was breathing hard.

"Now, Bumpy," I started. But I was interrupted by Elease now entering the room.

"He did the same thing to me, too, Daddy," she said in a loud voice and a twinkle in her eyes. "Patted me right on the butt and said he couldn't wait to get me alone. And it's not the first time he did it!"

"Elease!" I shouted. "And you didn't think to tell me anything, either? I find this all a little hard to believe." I turned back to Bumpy, but he was already heading toward the door. I tried to jump in front of him but Bumpy roughly pushed me out the way and I fell to the floor. I don't think he even noticed. He was in another world, and I knew Flash was in a world of trouble. Messing with Bumpy's money was bad enough, messing with his women folk was a whole other matter.

I confronted Ruthie and Elease, but they stuck to their stories. The timing was suspicious, but I knew that Flash was a real whoremonger, so it may have been true. At the same time, I just never could believe that Flash would disrespect Bumpy like that.

I ran downstairs and jumped into a cab and rushed to the Theresa Hotel. The taxi pulled up just as Bumpy was climbing out of his Cadillac. Flash was just coming out of the Theresa, and when he saw Bumpy he waved and started walking toward him. He must have noticed the look on Bumpy's face because he said, "What happened, Boss Man? Some shit went down we gotta take care of?"

Bumpy never said a word, he just hauled off and punched Flash in the face, propelling him back into the doorway of the Theresa. Before Flash could figure out what hit him, Bumpy was all over him, pummeling him viciously and cursing him the whole time.

"You lousy motherfucking no good nigger. I trust you in my house and you turn around and fucking shit on me? I'm gonna kill you!" Bumpy shouted as he beat Flash down onto the sidewalk. I felt paralyzed, and so did everyone else on the street. We had all seen fights before, but the sheer ferocity of the beating was horrifying. I thought he was going to really beat Flash to death right there on Seventh Avenue in broad daylight. Flash never raised a hand back at Bumpy, which was strange, because Flash was no punk. Maybe

169

it was because he knew he did wrong. Maybe it was because he knew he'd never be able to beat Bumpy anyway. Maybe it was because he couldn't bring himself to raise a hand to the man he loved as a father. Maybe it was all three, or none of the three; I'll never know. What I do know is that by the time Bumpy's rage had somewhat calmed Flash was lying in the gutter between two parked cars -- his face was unrecognizable.

Bumpy stood above him, breathing hard for a moment, before delivering one last kick to Flash's head and saying. "Stay away from me and my family else I'm gonna fucking kill you next time." Bumpy then slowly walked back to his car, but paused for a moment before climbing in. I thought, just for a moment, that he was going to turn back around and see if Flash was alright, but then his body slightly quivered, as if physically trying to shake off any regret, and he got in the car and drove off.

I hailed another cab and headed home, sick to my stomach at what I had just witnessed, but also with a feeling of dread. Something told me this wasn't the end, and the finish was going to be terrible for everyone involved.

When I got back to the house I found Ruthie and Elease in their room giggling. I went in and sat on Ruthie's bed and told them what happened, giving as much detail as I could so they could understand the gravity of the matter. They were shocked into silence. Then I stood up. "Of course if what you young ladies said is true then Flash deserved what he got. And of course I believe you, just like your father believes you. There would be hell to pay if he finds out different, but I'm not worried because I know you'd never lie about something as serious as this. And I know you're both smart enough to make sure your father never had reason to think you lied." I left it at that. I had to. If they were lying they were going to have to live with the lie, and if they weren't -- then like I said, Flash deserved what he got. And what was done was already done.

Bumpy knew those girls were no angels. Elease was downright wild, and was always hanging around grown men, flirting and carrying on. At one point she had the hots for the boxer Sugar Ray Robinson, and was always sneaking off and going to his club on 125th Street so she could be in his face, even though she knew both he and his wife were good friends of ours. Poor Sugar Ray didn't know how to handle it. I'm not saying he wasn't a womanizer, but he knew better than to try and womanize one of Bumpy's daughters, and he didn't want to be accused of doing something he wasn't doing, so he would call me or Bumpy and tell us to come get her. Bumpy would hop in his car, drag Elease out the club and beat her ass, but the beatings never seemed to take. She was sneaking off with older men, boys her own age, and it seemed like anyone who wore pants. Just a few months after the incident with Flash, Elease gave birth to a beautiful little girl whom we named Margaret, but not before Bumpy arranged a shotgun wedding, and likely to the wrong guy.

Ruthie was quieter, but my daughter had her moments. She was sneaky, and would lie in wait and then say things in an innocent manner that would instigate some kind of fight or argument, and then play like she didn't know how everything got started. She wasn't wild like Elease, but the two were buddies, and I knew that Ruthie helped Elease plan some of her wild outings just to get to me and Bumpy.

No, my girls were no angels.

Bumpy didn't come home that night, and when he did get home the next day he was very quiet. Flash was calling every hour on the hour trying to talk to

Bumpy, but Bumpy would pick up the phone and when he heard Flash's voice he would just hang up, and he instructed everyone else in the house to do the same. I could see he was really hurting over the Flash thing, but he didn't say anything about it, and I was afraid to bring it up.

Bumpy's friends, however, weren't as shy.

"Man, you know damn well you shoulda went ahead and killed that little nigga if you was going to beat him like that," I overhead Junie Byrd tell him a couple of days later when they were playing cards. "Shit, an ass kicking like that, in front of everyone, he ain't gonna forget that shit. You done made an enemy for life."

"Like I give a fuck," Bumpy said in a menacing voice. "The little motherfucker knows better than to try and cross me."

"I'm with Junie on this one," Finley said. "I'd lay odds that he's gonna come back at you. Why don't you go ahead and take care of him."

"Mind your business, man," Bumpy replied. "I did what I had to do and it's over."

"Shit ain't over," Nat Pettigrew said with a growl. "That nigga knows too much. If you ain't gonna take care of him I will. I ain't going down 'cause some punk wants to get back at you. I never did trust that little motherfucker."

Bumpy lay down his cards and looked at his old friend and said in a quiet voice. "I *said* the shit is over. Ain't nobody gonna take care of nobody."

But Nat didn't back down. "Bumpy, man, you know I got too much to lose."

"Wanna start your losses now?" Bumpy snapped.

The room got quiet, and I wondered what was going to happen next. Out of all of Bumpy's friends,

Nat was the most dangerous. Bumpy had counted on Flash for small matters, and he used him as a bodyguard and an enforcer, but when there was real trouble going down, it was always Nat who rode with Bumpy. He had no problem with knifing, strangling or shooting, and he knew how to make people disappear. He and Bumpy had never butted heads, and there was no telling what would happen if they did. They were known as the toughest men in Harlem, and it was more than just a reputation, it was the truth. Finley finally broke the tension. "If y'all niggas is gonna start shooting each other wait until the next hand. I'm working on a flush here, motherfuckers."

We all started laughing, and the card game resumed. But everyone knew where Nat was coming from and why he was concerned.

Heroin had hit New York, and had hit Harlem bad. The Italians were the ones who brought the dope in, but they didn't have the connects to peddle it, so they approached Bumpy who by right they had to approach about everything in Harlem first. Bumpy didn't want anything to do with junk, and told them so in no uncertain terms. So they started approaching other blacks with connections in Harlem, and one of the ones who bit was Nat Pettigrew. By 1950, Nat was making a mint selling smack, and Freddie Parsons wasn't far behind. To my knowledge Junie never got involved, and of course Finley's hustle was gambling and women, but many of Bumpy's associates got rich off white powder.

Bumpy never sold heroin, but that didn't mean he wasn't making a bunch of money off of it. Like everyone else involved in criminal activity in Harlem, the dope dealers had to kick back a portion of their money to Bumpy in order to operate, and in addition, Bumpy also loaned them money – at 25 percent interest

– when they were short on cash and needed to buy weight.

There were never any packages of dope in our apartment, but there were plenty of packages of money. If someone called and wanted to get some cash in a hurry when Bumpy was on his way out, he packaged up the thousand dollars or whatever they needed and left it with me or Flash to give it to the person when they showed up. They'd ring the bell, I'd bring the package to the door and they'd leave.

That's what Bumpy's friends meant when they said Flash knew too much.

Ed Smalls was also worried. He called Bumpy to his house in Sugar Hill shortly after that card game, and when Bumpy got there he sat him down and told him that he needed to go ahead and make up with Flash.

"Bumpy, you know you love that boy like a son, and he loves you like a father. It doesn't make any sense you not talking to him. He's torn up behind that shit."

Bumpy tried to wave him off, saying that he respected Ed, but it wasn't really none of his business. But Ed was persistent.

"You can't leave it the way it is. That boy is going around telling everyone how hurt he is, and I know you well enough to know you're hurt, too, even if you're too bullheaded to admit it," he said.

"I'll take care of it when I'm ready," Bumpy answered.

"Well, I hope you're ready now," Smalls said as he stood up.

"What do you mean?"

"He's in the other room."

Bumpy jumped up and made like he was going to go storming through the house looking for Flash, but Smalls stopped him.

"No, ain't gonna be no more beating up. Either you make up with him in this house here and now, or you take him out of here and take care of the situation for real."

It was clear what Ed Smalls meant. Bumpy didn't say another word, he just left out the house. When he got home he told me what happened, and for the first time I pleaded with Bumpy to go ahead and at least talk to Flash to see if maybe they could work something out. Bumpy got so mad at me I thought he was going to hit me.

I really think that Bumpy was eventually going to relent and talk to Flash, but it would have to be when he was ready, and not because people were telling him to do so. And I also believe that Bumpy didn't think that Flash would ever turn on him in the meantime. I thought the same thing.

Then one of the girls that Flash used to run with, Lovey, stopped by to visit. She and Flash had broken up like a year before, but we stayed friendly and she would drop in from time to time just to talk. I let her in, of course, and we were having tea and sandwiches, but I noticed she was nervous, and kept looking at her watch. Finally she said, "Miss Mayme, what time is your husband going to be home?"

I told her not until the last number was out, and they had set aside the money to pay the winners, sometime about four-thirty. It was about four-fifteen then.

"Well, Miss Mayme, I need to talk to your husband, but I don't want him to be mad at me."

I said, "Child, why would Bumpy get mad at you? You're not trying to bring him no message from Flash are you?"

All of a sudden Lovey burst out in tears. "No, Miss Mayme. I ain't got no message from Flash. And I hope you won't tell him I was here."

"Well, why would I do that? I don't even speak to the man no more. You know that."

Just then Bumpy came in, and the girl really started blubbering. We both tried to calm her down, and finally she was composed enough to tell us a story that chilled us to the bone.

Flash had visited her a few days before, and told her he wanted her to come to our house for a visit, and slip a package of heroin underneath one of the sofa cushions when no one was looking. She was then supposed to report to Flash exactly where she stashed the heroin so he could call the cops.

Bumpy's face turned ashen, and I almost fainted. Bumpy quickly pulled himself together, thanked Lovey, and gave her a couple hundred dollars and told her to get on the next train out of town so Flash wouldn't be able to find her. He also told her that when she got settled that she should give me a call and let me know where she was, and if she needed any more money it would be taken care of.

As soon as she left, Bumpy got on the telephone and called Nat, Steve, Obadiah, Junie, Ritchie, Georgie, Hoss, and Finley. Within minutes they were all gathered in my living room, and they were all strapped. They talked for about a half hour in low voices, and then they all walked out the door together. They were going hunting for Flash.

But it was already too late.

.

Chapter Nine – An Unjust Bust

That day in May 1951 started off like every other morning. Bumpy awoke at 5 a.m., as was his routine, and I got up and fixed him his usual morning drink – a beaten raw egg in a glass of cold milk. The baby, Margaret, was up early so I fixed her a quick breakfast as Bumpy dressed, and then gave him a quick kiss as he was getting ready to walk out the door and start his day.

"Mayme, if you have the laundry packed I'll drop it off since I have to run over to Seventh Avenue," he told me.

"You sure, Bumpy? I don't mind taking it."

"Don't make no sense for you to do that since I'll be stopping right next to the place," he assured me.

I gave him the large black laundry bag, he slung it over his back, and headed out.

We were still living at 120th Street, and his black Cadillac was parked in its usual spot, right across the street from the apartment building. He told me he noticed a black Ford cruising up the street, but paid it no mind. He put the laundry in the backseat, and climbed in the front seat and was ready to take off when the Ford pulled up in front of him.

There were two men inside, he later told me he recognized one of them. It was this guy James Chappell, who everyone in Harlem knew was a narcotics agent. Bumpy told me he wasn't that upset when he saw Chappell, because he was clean, and he didn't have anything on him but a numbers pad to write his numbers.

Over the past few weeks before various drug enforcement agents had tried to entrap him, telling him they wanted to score from him, but he would just laugh in their face. This one guy, his name was Newkirk, was really persistent, though. He followed Bumpy around and kept popping up all the time and approaching Bumpy about buying drugs. One time Bumpy had our granddaughter, Margaret in the car. She wasn't even one-years-old, but Bumpy used to love taking her around. They didn't have baby car seats back then, but Bumpy would place her in a basket and put her in the front seat and buckle the seat belt around the basket all snug and drive her around all day, bringing her to Smalls, or Lump's, or one of the other spots showing her off. Bumpy loved kids, and he just adored Margaret. She was his little jewel.

So he had taken Margaret over to Frazier's and let everyone make a fuss over her, and then he loaded her back in the car to bring her home so she could take her afternoon nap. It was in early May, and the weather was warm, so he opened her window a little so she could get some air, put his keys in the ignition and was about to take off when this Newkirk guy stuck his head in the car window. Like I said, he had been pestering Bumpy for weeks, but Bumpy would just laugh him off and leave it like that because he didn't want to give the police any reason to run him in since it was obvious they were trying to pin something on him. But see Newkirk didn't put his head in the driver's side window, his hear was in the passenger window instead. And little Margaret was in there. Before Newkirk could say two words Bumpy told him, "If you don't get your head out this car I'm going to knock it off for you." The Newkirk guy was shocked, because Bumpy had never spoke like that to him, but he knew Bumpy's reputation, and he pulled his head out that car quick. Didn't bother Bumpy again, either.

So when Chappell pulled up in front of his car that morning when Bumpy was getting ready to take off with the laundry, Bumpy was kind of surprised. Chappell was never one to bother him, and they actually had a decent kind of relationship. They'd see each other in the street, nod at each other, and then go on their separate ways.

So Chappell drives up with this other guy in the car and says, "Hey Bumpy. Where you going?"

Bumpy just looked at him and said, "I got a number pad. You want that?"

Chappell shook his head. "We want you downtown at the Narcotics Bureau."

"You don't want me in no Narcotics Bureau."

Chappell got out his car and said, "The Bureau says they want you. And they sent me down here to get you. It would be nice if you didn't start any trouble."

Bumpy said Chappell looked kind of nervous, so he just said, "Let me just go upstairs and tell my wife and family that I'm under arrest."

Chappell said he'd have to go with him, so all three of them came upstairs. I was surprised when Bumpy came in, and at first I thought he'd forgotten something, but then I noticed the two men with him.

"Mayme," Bumpy said, "I'm getting run in. Call the lawyer and let him know," and then he gave me a kiss on the cheek. I wasn't worried at that point, because I thought it was just another numbers beef. Bumpy had his car keys in his hand, and was jingling them when he was talking to me. So then he turns to Chappell and says, "Okay, let's go." But then the other agent reaches out and snatches the keys from Bumpy and says, "We'll take these if you don't mind."

Wel,l why did he do that? Bumpy snatched the keys back The agent acted like he was getting ready to make a move on Bumpy so Bumpy pulled his arm way back, and he was going to lay a very serious haymaker on the guy, but Chappell pushed the guy out of the way just in time.

"Bumpy," Chappell said, "I thought you said you were going to play nice."

"Fuck that," Bumpy said, "Don't no one be snatching nothing out my hand. And in my house? Aw, hell no."

Bumpy had to be really upset to be cursing like that. Don't get me wrong, Bumpy was good for cursing, but he had ground rules. He didn't believe anyone should curse in front of a lady they didn't know well, and they shouldn't curse in front of their wife when there were men around who didn't know her well, because that kind of gave them permission to curse in front of her. And for him to get ready to fight a police person in the house with me and Margaret there . . . well, now I started getting scared. Something was up, and suddenly this didn't feel like just the usual numbers arrest.

Chappell kept trying to calm Bumpy down, but I was too frazzled to help him out. I was still trying to figure out exactly what was going on.

Finally Chappell said there was no reason for Bumpy to give up the keys, and in fact Bumpy could drive himself down to the Bureau, and he would ride with Bumpy while the other agent took their car. The other agent tried to protest, but Chappell told him, "Man, will you just shut up and let me handle this?"

Bumpy calmed down and gave me another kiss, and I whispered in his ear, "What's going on, Bumpy." But he just smiled and chucked me under the chin and said for me not to fret, just call the lawyer and tell him where he was. He never did tell me that they were taking him down to the Narcotics Bureau. He didn't want me to worry.

180

As soon as they left I got on the phone and tried to call his lawyer, a Jewish guy named Lindenbauer, but couldn't find him. He was probably holed up with this honey he was crazy about who lived in Sugar Hill. Everyone knew Lindenbauer was making a fool of himself over the girl, and he finally left his wife for her and committed suicide when the girl didn't want him anymore. Anyway, he was in the midst of still trying to get with the girl during this time, and that's probably where he was, with her. If I had known where she lived I would have gone over there and pulled him out of bed to take care of Bumpy, but I didn't know where she lived, so I just kept leaving messages with his secretary. Then I called Junie, Steve Mitchell and Finley, and tried to get Nat on the phone but couldn't find him either. Junie, Steve, and Finley came right over and I told them everything that happened.

"Man, you got me up out my bed at seven in the morning just 'cause Bumpy got pinched on a numbers rap?" Finley growled. "Shit, I'm going back home."

But Junie said, "It don't sound right to me. What you think, Steve?"

Steve shook his head. "Man, Chappell wouldn't be in on no numbers bust. This is some serious shit."

I asked him what he meant, and that's when I found out for the first time that Chappell was hooked up with the Narcotics Bureau. It took all the strength I had not to fall to pieces right then. Now even Finley started looking concerned. The guys left and told me not to worry; they'd take care of everything, but for me to keep trying to get the lawyer. Right after they left, Freddy Parsons came over to the house to drop off his numbers and numbers money for me to put in the dresser drawer. Freddy was a young guy, the same age as Flash, and they had been good friends. In fact, it was Flash that got him the job running numbers for Bumpy.

Even after Bumpy and Flash fell out Bumpy kept Freddy around because, after all, Freddy had done nothing wrong.

So when Freddy comes over he's acting all nervous, and was all sweaty, and couldn't look me in the eye. He gave me the money, and was heading out the door when he turned around and dug a watch that Bumpy had loaned him out of his pocket and gave it to me.

I said, "Well, I won't be able to give it to Bumpy for awhile, because they arrested him this morning."

Freddy really started sweating then and said, "Yeah, I know. Flash told me. He's over on the Avenue telling everyone he got Bumpy pinched."

I was shocked, but I made like I knew what he was talking about just so he could tell me more. So I said, "Yeah, that damn Flash. I always knew he was no good. And now he done turned on Bumpy."

Freddy nodded and said, "Miss Mayme, when they pulled me in last night I didn't know what was going on. I swear I didn't. They started telling me all this stuff Flash told them and said they just wanted me to back up his story. If Flash had been there right then I would have jumped on him on the spot. They kept me there all night questioning me. I just got out this morning and was heading over here to warn Bumpy when I ran into Flash and he boasted that Bumpy had already been picked up. So I just went ahead and collected my numbers so I could come over here and give you the money in case you needed it."

"But you were just getting ready to walk out and not tell me anything, Freddy? How's that? What exactly did you say to those people?"

Freddy looked like he was gonna cry. "I didn't tell them anything, Miss Mayme. They told me Flash had told them all this stuff but I just said I didn't know what they were talking about. I swear!"

I told him I believed him, and said for him to just go in the dining room because I was going to fix him a big breakfast, considering everything he'd been through. Then I went into the bedroom and called Junie, Steve, and Finley, but there was no answer. I guess they were all out in the street getting the information I had just been given in my living room. Then I tried Nat again, but still couldn't reach him. When I went back in the dining room Freddy was gone. I've never seen him again.

Lindenbauer finally called me back at six that evening. He made some calls to find out what was going on and then phoned me back and said Bumpy was being charged with selling drugs.

Now, I know there's people that say gangster's wives don't always know all the stuff their men are into, but those people don't know what they're talking about. Girlfriends might not know, but wives do – at least back then. When a woman is deemed good enough to be moved from the ranks of girlfriend to wife, then that means the man trusts her all the way. He tells her things he wouldn't tell anyone else, because she has to know what's going on so she can handle any situation that has to be handled if her man gets pinched. I knew about all of Bumpy's number spots, all the gambling houses, the people to whom he loansharked, all the night clubs who paid for protection (okay, some people might call it extortion), and I knew that Bumpy didn't sell no drugs! He and I might have argued about it (maybe!), but he would have told me if for no reason than that I would have to know to get rid of any stash he had if was arrested. So how could they tell me he was arrested for selling drugs? Now it would be different if they got him on loaning drug dealers money, because I already mentioned all the money packages Bumpy would leave at the house for someone to pick up. But selling drugs? No.

Junie came back to the apartment and I told him about Freddy's visit, and the Lindenbauer's phone call, but he already knew everything. He told me he was going to take me down to Federal Detention Center on West Street so we could bail Bumpy out, but just then Lindenbauer called and said that Bumpy wouldn't be arraigned until the morning, and that they weren't allowing him to see anyone.

We went down the next morning. Bumpy's bail was set at $25,000. I had that and more at the house, but Lindenbauer said that if I turned over cash it would make the Feds suspicious, so I called Bumpy's sister, Margie. Bumpy had set her up with real estate investments for just this kind of emergency, though Lord knows we thought we might have to use the collateral on an assault or extortion charge or something, not drugs. So, anyway, we planned on putting up one of her houses as collateral. We agreed to meet at the bail bondman's office the next day to get everything arranged.

Well, wouldn't you know Nat finally called me that afternoon and said he'd been out of town and had just heard what happened. He asked me how much the bail was and I told him, and before I could say another word he said, "Don't worry. I got the cash right here. I'll go get him bailed out right now." I tried to tell him to wait, but he'd already hung up and when I tried to call him back there was no answer. He'd already left.

You wouldn't believe what happened next! Nat went down there with $25,000 in a brown paper bag – I don't know why, but Nat never used a wallet; he always carried his money in a paper bag -- and when he got to the place to put the money up and gave them his name the Fed said, "Nat Pettigrew? Yeah, well, we were looking for you. You're under arrest."

It wasn't funny, but it sure was funny. When Junie told me what happened we all cracked up. Then the next day we bailed both Bumpy and Nat out of jail.

It turns out that Flash had been arrested for selling like an ounce of heroin in December of 1950, and when they picked him up he told them that he was selling the drugs for Bumpy. Well, their ears perked up, and they said if that was the case maybe they could cut him a deal. Well Flash sang like a canary. A lying canary. He said that Bumpy sent him to get a package from some Italian guys on the East Side, and then had him sell the package to someone else – and that someone else turned out to be an undercover guy. But when some of the Narcotics guys came in later that night they told their superiors that Flash was full of crap. That with all the things they heard on the street they'd never heard that Bumpy was in the drugs trade. Well, their superiors got all up in arms and kind of insinuated that maybe they were saying that because they were on Bumpy's payroll. That's when Chappell spoke up and said, "Well, how about this? Bumpy and Flash hate each other since Bumpy beat his brains out in front of the Theresa Hotel in October. There's no way Bumpy would trust Flash with selling drugs for him."

That threw everyone for a loop, especially when they started asking around and found out it was true. They got so mad at Flash for lying they were going to throw the book at him when the Feds stepped in and said even if Bumpy didn't sel,l they knew he knew all of the big time dealers in Harlem, and if they could make the charges against Bumpy stick they could get him to flip on the dealers and clean up the drug trade in Harlem. So, Flash amended his story and said that he wasn't selling drugs for Bumpy that particular time, but had sold for him in the past. The Feds were ecstatic, but knowing that the Flash story might not hold up in court, they went about trying to set Bumpy up – which was why they sent Newkirk sniffing around.

The case was crazy. They even persuaded some poor guy – Horace Cartwright, a heroin user who was arrested for selling a half-ounce of heroin to an undercover agent -- to say that he was also selling the drugs for Bumpy. Funny thing was that Hoss Cartwright, who used to run with Red Dillard Morrison and Fess Taylor did deal drugs, but not this Horace Cartwright guy.

Bumpy didn't trust Lindenbauer with the case because he was still mooning over that girl in Sugar Hill, so he hired this hot-shot lawyer named Henry Lowenberg. Bumpy spent a small fortune on that case, and Lowenberg filed motion after motion, trying to get the case thrown out of court, but the Feds wouldn't let go. The federal prosecutor, William O'Brien, even made all the New York papers when he called Bumpy "the most dangerous man in New York."

The Feds kept badgering Bumpy, saying if he would just give them some names the whole thing would be over but Bumpy told them to take a flying leap. Roy Cohn, who became famous during the McCarthy hearings, was working in the Manhattan federal prosecutors at the time. He told Bumpy that he was stupid to risk going to jail for life in order to protect someone, and then added "But I guess that's how you darkies are; loyal to the point of stupidity." At that point Bumpy jumped out of his chair and lunged at the lawyer but was held back. He yelled at him, "If you ever say anything like that again, I'm going to throw you out the window, you little punk." Years later, it became known that Cohn was actually a closeted homosexual and Bumpy told his friend "Spanish" Raymond Marquez that had he known it at the time he would never have called Cohn a punk. He wanted to kill him, but he hadn't intended to make fun of him.

Lowenberg kept getting the actual case postponed with all the motions he was filing – and when Hawk shot Bumpy in 1952 it further delayed the trial. It wasn't until June of 1953 that we finally went to trial. The whole time Bumpy was out on bail he was really confident that he would be found not guilty, and even more so when the trial began. Lowenberg was great, and caught witness after witness in lies, and Horace Cartwright – that poor guy – actually admitted that he didn't even know Bumpy. He said on the stand he didn't know anything about how to sell heroin, and that a friend of his had introduced him to a man who said he'd pay twenty bucks to score some heroin for him. So he went to guy whom he always bought his own personal drugs and hooked the guy up. The man turned out to be an undercover agent and said they'd go easy on him if he said Bumpy was his dealer.

Then an undercover agent got on the stand and said he'd bought heroin from Bumpy himself, and Bumpy had sold it to him right in a restaurant. Now how could they be calling Bumpy a big time heroin dealer when he would actually take a risk by selling to some guy he didn't know $435 worth of heroin in a restaurant? Come on. Bumpy spent almost two hundred thousand dollars on his defense, and this was back in 1947. He was selling $435 worth of heroin in a restaurant? What do you think?

Then Flash got on the stand and said that he'd been a drug courier for Bumpy since 1949. He even said that since him and Bumpy fell out that he'd been working as an electrical inspector for an elevator company downtown. Now, you know, if Flash had been anywhere around in New York City, Bumpy's crew would have found him, and then this whole thing would never have happened. In fact, Flash later admitted in the African-American newspaper The New York Age, that the feds had put him in protective custody. And Flash an electrical inspector? Flash never even finished school. Lowenberg was able to punch all kinds of holes in Flash's testimony.

Then Lowenberg put Lovey Hamilton on the stand, and she told them how Flash had it in for Bumpy and how he tried to get her to plant drugs under one of the cushions in our sofa.

The trial lasted three days, and the whole time Bumpy and Lowenberg were confident that Bumpy would be let off. On that third day, after closing arguments, we all went and had lunch. Bumpy and Lowenberg were talking about the trial and how well they thought it went, and Bumpy said he thought the judge, his name was Edward Dimock was pretty fair. He said that he could look at Dimock's face and see that he wasn't even buying all the lies that the prosecution witnesses were telling.

The jury was only out for three hours before it was announced they'd reached a verdict, and Lowenberg said he thought that was a good sign because juries are usually out longer when they're going to find a defendant guilty. I was still nervous and uneasy, and told Bumpy I didn't think I could go in the courtroom to hear the verdict because I would die if they found him guilty. He laughed and kissed me and said for me to stop worrying, just wait outside the courtroom and he'd be back in just a few minutes and then we'd all go back uptown and have dinner at the Shalimar.

They all went in, and five minutes later Lovey Hamilton came running out and grabbed me by the

188

shoulders. "Mayme," she said. "They said he's guilty."
I let out a scream that echoed throughout the courthouse.

We'd driven down to the courthouse that day with a carload of friends, but Bumpy told everyone that they had to find another way back home because he needed to talk to me privately. When we got in the car he ranted and raved for awhile about the injustice of it all, then he got quiet for awhile and I asked him what he was thinking.

"Mayme, you should have seen the judge. I think he was just as shocked as me when the jury found me guilty. He knew I was innocent."

I just nodded, wondering where he was going with all this.

Then he said, "In fact, I think he likes me. They wanted to revoke my bail and haul me off to prison right after they announced the verdict, and the judge said no way. Said that I should be given time to get my affairs in order."

"That was good of him."

"Yeah. In fact, I'm thinking about reaching out to him."

"What do you mean?"

"I'm thinking if I offer him a little gift. You know, just a little something. Maybe ten thousand or twenty thousand or so, and ask him to go light on the sentencing."

"What? Do you really think that might work?" I asked.

Bumpy shrugged. "I don't know. But it can't hurt to try. Shit. I was found guilty on two counts of drug trafficking. That could be fifteen years each. I'd be an old man before I got out. I might be dead."

"But, Bumpy," I said, "that's so risky. What if he turns you in? Then you'd get even more time."

Bumpy slammed his fist down on the steering wheel. "It's worth the risk. I'm not trying to do no thirty years. If I hit him up right maybe I can convince him to just give me probation."

"With your record?" I said skeptically.

"Yeah, well I ain't never been convicted for no damn drugs. Maybe he could just sentence me to four or five years and let me do the rest on probation. I could do that no problem. You think twenty thousand would be enough?"

"I still think it's too risky. Maybe you should talk this over with Lowenberg?"

Bumpy shook his head. "No. Ain't no use getting him involved in this. I'll reach out to him on my own. I'll find a way."

That night, Nat, Junie, Steve Mitchell, Finley, Ritchie Williams, Obadiah, and Wesley Goodwin all met at the house with Bumpy. The whole crew was there, even Ed Smalls who wasn't part of the crew but thought of Bumpy as a son. They sat down, and then Bumpy told them what he'd already told me, that he was going to bribe the judge. Nat immediately went for it, because he'd also been found guilty, and he was hoping for a break. The others talked about it for about an hour, and they finally agreed it was worth the risk. Ed Smalls was like me, he didn't like the idea. Then he added that he thought it would take a lot more than twenty thousand dollars to make it worth the judge's while.

"How much you think it'll take?" Bumpy asked him.

"I wouldn't even think of offering him less than a hundred thousand if I were you," Ed answered.

"Damn, that much!" Bumpy said.

Ed nodded. "Don't worry. I'll cover whatever you can't scrape up."

190

"Naw, I got it, man," Bumpy said. "This is my problem not yours." He turned to Nat. "You putting up half, right?"

"Shit. I'll put up the whole thing if you think it'll work."

"No, it's for both of us. I got my half right here in the house. How long before you can get yours?"

"I got mine in my apartment, too. I'll bring it over tomorrow."

Ed Smalls said he'd ask around and find out where the judge lived. "But, Bumpy, you gotta insulate yourself."

"What do you mean?" Bumpy asked.

"Just in case the judge is a straight arrow and turns you down you don't want to be in a position where he can turn you in for attempted bribery."

"So how should I handle it?"

Ed shook his head. "Give me a day or so and I'll figure something out."

Ed Smalls was as good as his word. Not only did he insulate Bumpy, he insulated himself. He paid one of his guys $5,000 to reach out to one of his guys for $2,000 to find someone close to the judge who could be trusted. That person turned out to be the judge's driver. A couple of days later Bumpy drove over to the judge's house in Long Island with a suitcase with $100,000. But when he got there the driver met him in the driveway and told him to turn around and go home. When Bumpy asked him why, the man told him that while he was driving Dimock around the day before he casually asked him if he thought a judge might be willing to reduce a man's sentence for a $100,000. The judge whistled and said that was a lot of money, and he didn't know many judges who would turn something like that down. Then the driver said he knew a guy who was in that position, and that he wanted to go to the judge in his case and bring him the money the next day. Dimock said, "One hundred thousand cash, huh? Like I said, that's a lot of money." The driver took that as the judge being willing to do Bumpy the sentencing favor. But then when he mentioned to the judge that morning that his visitor was on the way, Dimock asked what visitor was he talking about. He didn't have any appointments that day. The driver reminded him of the conversation they'd had in the car and the judge got red in the face, then exploded and fired him on the spot.

Bumpy asked him if the judge knew it was him that he'd been talking about and the driver said no, he'd never mentioned Bumpy's name. Bumpy got in the car and drove back to Harlem.

I don't know if Dimock is still alive – probably not, because he was old even then – but his family can feel good that they were related to a man who couldn't be bought. Not even for one hundred thousand in tax-free dollars. It didn't make me feel good, though. And it didn't make Bumpy feel good. A few days later the judge sentenced him to fifteen years -- ten years on one count, and five years on the other. To run consecutively, which meant Bumpy had to do a total of fifteen years.

So in June 1953, Bumpy was hauled off to prison. He appealed the verdict all the way to the U. S. Supreme Court, but they refused to hear the case. Bumpy had done a lot of prison time over his life, but this was the only time he was bitter. He was now a convicted drug dealer. He never got over it. Never.

Chapter Ten – Return of the King

Bumpy wound up doing a total of ten years before finally being let out in 1963 on Mandatory Release. He would have done more time than that if his friends hadn't stepped in. See, in addition to the fifteen years in prison, Bumpy was also sentenced to pay $9,000 in fines. Do you know my stubborn behind husband refused to pay even though it meant he wouldn't be eligible for parole? He said he'd be damned if he paid a fine for a crime he didn't commit. I pleaded with him, Junie pleaded with him, everyone pleaded him but Bumpy wouldn't budge. Ed Small even offered to pay the whole fine himself so Bumpy could get back on the street, but Bumpy wouldn't hear of it. To him, paying the fine would be admitting he did the crime.

Even prison officials told Bumpy to just pay the money and get the hell out – Bumpy was far from a model prisoner, and I'm sure they couldn't wait to get rid of him. He got dozens of write-ups while in prison, mostly for disobedience and fighting, and he spent more than half his time in solitary which suited him just fine. He'd get out in general population for awhile, then be back in solitary in no time. Prison correspondence indicated that the main problem the officials had with him was his influence over the black inmates. The official said that the blacks treated Bumpy as if he were their leader, and that since Bumpy was "overly sensitive – to the point of obsession" about race issues other inmates were now also too touchy about things that hadn't bothered them before Bumpy's arrival.

Bumpy's first prison stop was the Federal Penitentiary in Leavenworth, Kansas, in June 1953. In a

193

report dated March 15, 1954 written by the warden read in part:

"Information contained in the subject's jacket indicates that his regarded as a bombastic, egocentric extrovert of superior intelligence, but possessing an unstable personality and having assaultive tendencies."

In April 1954, Bumpy was transferred to Alcatraz – where the other federal pens sent their most dangerous criminals or inmates deemed incorrigible. Bumpy had more than a few brushes with the authorities his first couple of years there, but eventually he seemed to settle in and get along well. His philosophy was "If they leave me alone, I'll leave them alone," and they eventually began to respect that. He was even given a meritorious award for helping to calm things down when a race riot threatened to break out. In 1958 he requested a transfer to Lewisburg so he could have more visits - inmates were only allowed one visit a month at Alcatraz. He was instead transferred to the federal penitentiary in Atlanta that December. On April 14, 1959, the warden of the prison, F. T. Wilkinson wrote to the director of prisons:

"Following his transfer to this institution from the U. S. Penitentiary, Alcatraz, December 21, 1958, it did not take Johnson very long to get himself seriously involved with several members of our official staff. He has been regularly disobedient, hostile, resentful, and almost insanely race conscious."

The warden went on to say in that letter that unless Bumpy's attitude improved "appreciatively" that he'd probably be writing the director to recommend that Bumpy be transferred back to Alcatraz.

Well, only a few hours after the letter was put in the mail Bumpy and another inmate were brought into the warden's office for fighting. Bumpy was furious, because he and the inmate had been arguing over lunch, and decided that they were going to fight it out – but a fair one. But as Bumpy was sharpening two spoons for them to use as weapons the inmate "stole" on him; stabbing him in the chest with a spoon he had already pocketed. The warden was patiently trying to explain to Bumpy that both men needed to figure out another way to handle their disputes when the inmate – who was white – said there was just "no reasoning with niggers." Bumpy reached forward, picked up a heavy paperweight off the warden's desk and smashed it into the inmates face, breaking his nose. Bumpy was promptly put in the hole and that same day the warden sent out another letter to the director's office, stating:

"From the time of is arrival, we have had a series of incidents in which Johnson has gone into almost violent rage, has been continuously hypercritical of the rules and procedures at this institution, and has demanded from the onset a single cell. He has threatened personnel and inmates on several occasions and on one occasion when he was having a noisy, verbal altercation with the Rear Corridor Officer, with a number of inmates crowded around, I personally interfered to get him out of the corridor to avoid serious trouble. . . . We have been exceedingly patient and have confined him for a few days on several occasions after which we would turn him out in population, but usually the same day he would be in another violent quarrel. It appears we have no recourse but to recommend that he be returned to Alcatraz."

The director must have contacted the warden suggesting that if Bumpy were having so many problems he shouldn't be sent to Alcatraz because he might have mental issues that would worsen at such a strict institution. The warden then sent Bumpy for mental evaluation. The clinical psychologist, Laurence L. Bryan wrote in part:

"While he is very sensitive, resentful, and has rather strong ideas of racial persecution, I am convinced that he is entirely non-psychotic, and fully qualified, in so far as his mental condition is concerned, to be returned to the Alcatraz Island Penitentiary."

And so in September 1959, Bumpy was returned to Alcatraz. He was only there a month before he was put in segregation for fighting with another inmate.

It's ironic that out of all the prisons Bumpy seemed to get along best at Alcatraz, although that's the prison most dreaded by inmates. I think it's probably because all of the prisoners were hardened criminals who didn't take any bullshit and didn't give any. Everyone left everyone alone, and the guards – for the most part – didn't mess with inmates because they knew every single one of these guys were capable of extreme violence when pushed. Remember, Alcatraz was set up for prisoners considered too dangerous for other institutions, the inmates who were considered incorrigible, or were a flight risk

Bumpy was in Alcatraz on June 11, 1962 when Frank Morris, and two brothers Clarence and J. W. Anglin made the only successful escape from that high security institution. There had been other attempts at a prison break, but Alcatraz was supposed to the nation's only break-out proof prison. In addition to hourly cell checks by prison guards, Alcatraz was on an island in the middle of the San Francisco Bay, and a boat would be needed to get the mainland.

The escape was masterminded by Frank Morris another inmate named Alan West, and the plan was to somehow smuggle in tools to chip at the concrete in their cells, reach the vents to reach the roof of the prison, scale the walls, and make it to the beach and sail off in a homemade raft. The problem was smuggling in the tools, and the making of a sturdy enough raft to make it to the mainland. They used prison issued raincoats to make the raft, but they knew it wouldn't be sturdy enough to make it far into the bay. The other big problem was how to get around those hourly cell checks. That one they solved by making crude dummies and placing them in their cots so that when the guards passed by with their flashlights it looked like the men were inside sleeping.

On the night of the 12th they put their plan into action. West found the hole he had made in the cell wasn't big enough for him to get through, and he was ultimately left behind. Morris and the Anglin brothers made it to the beach, and to this day – despite a nationwide manhunt – their whereabouts have not been discovered.

There has been speculation that the escapees had to have had help from people on the outside who could smuggle in materials, and also arrange for a boat to meet them in the middle of the bay to get to the San Francisco shore. But prison officials agree that none of the men involved in the plot had those kind of strong outside connections. Well, maybe not any of the men they knew to be involved with the plot.

In his 1989 book, *Riddle of the Rock: The Only Successful Escape from Alcatraz*, author Don Nevi interviewed a former inmate – Joe Carnes – who said that when West told him about the plot, and wanted to know what inmate in the prison could they go to with strong enough outside connections to help with the escape. Carnes said he told them to solicit Bumpy.

Carnes said Bumpy later told him that he had indeed agreed to help out with the escape plot. It could be that Bumpy helped them even though he wasn't interested in escaping himself since he had no desire to live the life of a fugitive. Years later when I asked Bumpy about it, he simply winked and said, "West and I were friends, and you know I always try to help a friend – especially if the price is right." I didn't press him anymore about it, because I didn't really care. The only person I was interested in leaving Alcatraz was Bumpy.

When Alcatraz had to downsize to prepare for the permanent closing of the institution both Atlanta and Leavenworth made it clear they didn't want him, and in January 1963, Bumpy was eventually sent to Lewisburg, Pennsylvania where he had wanted to go in the first place.

Yes, I know all of this seems unbelievable, but it's all documented. How bad does an inmate have to be for even the prisons to try and get rid of him?

Bumpy was shocked when he was told in January 1963 that he was going to be released on Mandatory Parole also known as Mandatory Release. Mandatory Release is given to prisoners who have served two-thirds of their sentence and has not "seriously or frequently violated institution rules or regulations." You see why Bumpy was shocked, right? I was shocked, too! I mean, there was no doubt that Bumpy shouldn't have been eligible because of his infractions. But prison officials really, I mean, really wanted to cut Bumpy loose, and all of a sudden they gave him back all the good time he'd had taken away from him, and said he was a candidate for Mandatory Release. Then Bumpy told them he wouldn't take Mandatory Release if it meant he had to pay that fine. Now it was the prison officials turn to be shocked. But they suggested that Bumpy take what was known as a "Pauper's Oath," saying that he was indigent and couldn't pay the fine but would try to make good after he got out. Bumpy told them he wouldn't pay the fine even after he was released, but they told him to just go ahead and put in for the Pauper's Oath, and worry about everything else later.

By this time only $6,675 was left on the original $9,000 fine because Bumpy had made four $100 payments while out on bail, thinking at the time the money would be returned when he was found not guilty. Then when he was found guilty the Feds confiscated his Cadillac, and sold it for $1,925. Yes, in 1947 Cadillacs were a lot cheaper than they are today, but they were still a lot more expensive than that – but that's what the Feds said they were able to sell it for.

So Bumpy puts in for the Pauper's Oath, expecting it to be accepted and he'd get out on April 4, 1963. But then he gets a letter back saying the parole people asking how could it be that he was taking the Pauper's Oath when in the release plan he'd given prison officials he indicated that he was planning on spending $12,000 to set himself up in the chemical business making detergents. Bumpy wrote back and said he'd be partnering with friends to open the business and they would stake the money. Then they came back and said that they investigated and found that he had a balance of $1,503.14 on his commissary, or prison account. How could it be, they asked that he could have that much money in his account having spent ten years in prison and still say he was broke and had no way of getting money. Well, that was that, as far as Bumpy was concerned. He wasn't turning over a red hot dime on the fine.

His Mandatory Release date came and went and Bumpy was still sitting up in Lewisburg. That's when I went to see Bumpy and put my foot down – which simply means I cried and got hysterical, and Bumpy caved into my tears like always – and promised he'd get out on Mandatory Release. The new date was set for May 4th, but Bumpy still was fuming over having to pay the fine. Finally Junie and them said they were going to go ahead and make the monthly $100 payments, and for him to just get his ass out. Bumpy had to turn over his commissary money as a show of good faith, but on May 4th my husband was finally on his way home.

Bumpy flew into Newark Airport, and Junie went and picked him up in a 1962 Cadillac Eldorado convertible. Right after they crossed the George Washington Bridge there were about twenty carloads of people pulled alongside the road to greet him. Word had spread around Harlem of Bumpy's arrival, and there was an impromptu parade as Bumpy rode down Seventh Avenue, with the top of the convertible down. People were lined up on the sidewalk cheering and throwing confetti as the motorcade made its way through the streets of Harlem. Junie told me Bumpy had tears in his eyes as he stood up in the car and waved to the crowd. Bumpy later admitted that he thought the people of Harlem would have forgotten him after his long absence, or that they would treat him like a pariah because he was a convicted drug dealer. But you know, most of the people in Harlem knew Bumpy's reputation, and they had a hard time believing that Bumpy was selling drugs – no matter what some damn white jury said.

As for Flash, I have no idea whatever happened to him, but he wasn't seen around Harlem after Bumpy was sent away. I'm not even going to speculate as to why.

The plan was for Junie to drop Bumpy off at our apartment on 120th Street after they got back to Harlem, and I was there waiting for him, perfumed and in a sexy black negligee. I had arranged for Margaret, now 13, to stay at a friend's house; I was going to welcome my husband home in my own very special way. When I heard Bumpy's key in the door I placed a long stem red rose between my lips and struck up a sexy pose. Imagine my embarrassment when the door opened and there was Bumpy and about fifty other people staring at me. Mortified, I ran into the bedroom and immediately put on some decent clothes. By the time I got back into the living room the party was already going at full blast. It was about three o'clock in the morning before Bumpy and I had the opportunity to have our own private celebration.

I wasn't the only one ecstatic to have Bumpy home. Margaret had only been four when Bumpy went off to prison, and although I brought her along with me a few times when I visited Bumpy, now that he was back with us she couldn't get enough of him – or him of her. He took her around with him just like he did when she was baby. And he made it his business to take her to school in the morning and pick her up afterward. He really spoiled that child, but I guess he was always trying to make up for all the time he'd been away from her. Her birthday parties were community affairs, he'd actually close down the street and throw a mini-carnival in her honor – complete with rented ponies and rides that all the kids in the neighborhood could ride for free. And he had it set up so that whenever Margaret went to restaurants with her friends all she had to do was sign the check, and he'd pay it later.

Margaret called me mama and Bumpy daddy because we were really the only parents she knew, and in fact she thought we were her biological parents until she was about six. That's because Elease left New York shortly after Margaret was born, leaving her infant

201

daughter with us. We didn't mind. In fact, in 1951 we made plans to officially adopt Margaret, but the process back then was painstakingly slow, and midway through the process Bumpy was indicted and with all the newspaper attention, and the adoption agency turned us down. Elease would come around occasionally, and when she did I always tell Margaret "Give your mother a kiss," and she would do so. And when Elease sent Margaret gifts or dresses for her birthday, I would give them to Margaret and say, "Look what your mother bought you." But she never really made the connection, I guess. To her I was mama, Bumpy was daddy and Elease was just Elease.

But then when she was six-years-old Bumpy's sister was going over some lessons and Margaret didn't grasp the material fast enough for Genevieve's liking she snapped at Margaret and said she was stupid. I got angry, because I saw Genevieve was trying to destroy Margaret's self-esteem just as she did Elease's years ago when she was raising her. Like I said earlier, Genevieve wasn't the most nurturing person in the world, and sometimes could be downright mean.

"Ginny," I told her, "there's no need for you to be talking to the child like that."

To which Genevieve replied, "Don't tell me how to talk to her. You ain't her mother. You ain't even her blood."

Genevieve shoulda been glad Bumpy was in prison, because if he had heard her say that he would have blown a gasket. I stayed calm, though, and simply said, "And you're not her mother, either. If you can't say something nice to her, please don't say anything at all."

But after she left Margaret asked, "Why did she say you're not my mama?"

I sat her down and said, "Baby, Elease is your mother, but she's not able to be here right now. But I'm here, and I love you, and as far as I'm concerned I may not be your mother, but I'll always be your mama."

I could tell Margaret was still trying to make sense of it all, but she still continued to call me mama, and does to this day. And I never did forgive Genevieve for hurting her like that, though.

Anyway, it didn't take long for Bumpy to get back in the swing of things. He didn't reopen a numbers bank, but he still had about a dozen number spots that were still up and running even while he was in prison. That's where I got most of my money from while Bumpy was away, and that's the primary reason that Bumpy always had at least $1,000 in his prison commissary. That in addition to the fact that the whole time – and I do mean the whole time – that Bumpy was away a car would pull up in front of my building every month and an Italian guy would get out and bring me a bulging envelope full of money. Those guys knew that Bumpy could have sent the whole lot of them to prison forever, but he did his time like a man and never sang for the Feds. And the Italians appreciated it, and their appreciation kept those envelopes coming. And Bumpy's crew was always there for me, slipping me money even when I said I didn't need it and calling me two or three times a week to see if I wanted them to do anything for me. Console televisions had just come out right after Bumpy went away, and Steve Mitchell made sure he purchased a great big old Magnavox floor console for the apartment. Whenever Junie Byrd bought his wife a new mink he bought one for me, too. Margaret and I were well taken care of while Bumpy was away, and that's how it should be. I hear now about hustler's wives doing bad financially once their husbands get sent up, but I just don't understand how that can happen. It sure didn't happen to me.

In addition to the numbers spot, Bumpy decided to go into legitimate business. He opened up an exterminating business "Palmetto's Chemicals -- on Second Avenue, in East Harlem. There was a sign in the window of the shop that said, "We Get Rid of Pests."

Bumpy also entered into a partnership with Henry Perkins, who had opened up a restaurant and bar supply company on 146th Street and Amsterdam Avenue. Bumpy didn't know Perk before he was sent to prison, but after he got out he heard that Perk was a real standup guy whose business was struggling because people to whom he extended credit weren't paying. So Bumpy showed up at the Perk's company and said, "Maybe we can do business together. I need a supplier for my chemical store, and you need someone to make sure you get paid."

Perk was ecstatic. Having been born and raised in Harlem he, of course, knew of Bumpy's reputation. He immediately suggested they form a partnership. To celebrate their new partnership Bumpy suggested he and Perk go for a drive. They got into the car, and a half hour later they were in front of Margherite's Dugout – a popular club in Queens owned by Margherite Mays on Astoria Blvd. I'd known Margherite for years, and she was a real hustler. Startlingly beautiful, she married baseball great Willie Mays in 1956 when he was 25, and she was 35 or so. She lied to him about her age, and she told me he didn't pester her about it because he was so in love. "After I gave him oral sex the first time he was hooked for life," Margherite boasted to me. Willie Mays was a country boy from Alabama and Margherite was smooth talking beauty from Harlem. He never stood a chance. He was one of the highest paid ballplayers in the late fifties and early sixties, and Margherite went through his money like it was water. She made him buy a huge palatial home in New Rochelle, New York. Fifteen rooms and seven bedrooms, it was, and sat on one and a half acres. Then when they got into an argument because of her lavish spending and having friends over all the time she made him move out. He had to stay in a hotel room for a month before she finally agreed to reconcile. Margherite was a trip, but I liked her.

Perk at first didn't want to even go into the club because he'd had bad business relations with Margherite but before he could explain, Bumpy was out of the car and striding into the establishment so Perk followed.

"Where's Margherite?" Bumpy demanded of the woman wiping down the bar.

"She's not here. I think she's out of town," the woman haughtily replied.

Bumpy looked at her for a moment, turned to Perk and said, "Grab a couple of them empty boxes over there and put them on the bar."

Then Bumpy went around to the front of the bar and began taking full bottles of the top shelf liquors and placing them in the boxes.

"What are you doing?" the young woman yelled frantically.

"I'm helping Margherite pay off a debt," Bumpy said as he continued to fill the boxes. "When she gets back in town tell her I did her a favor."

The woman quickly disappeared into the back, and five minutes a later a car could be heard screeching to a halt in front of the club, and Margherite flew in, her hair in curlers and a coat pulled over a nightgown.

"Bumpy, I heard you were home. How are you doing?" Margherite said in the calmest voice she could muster under the circumstances.

"I'm doing fine," Bumpy said. "Perk, hand me another couple of boxes."

"So, why are you taking all of my liquor?"

Bumpy stopped for a moment and smiled. "You owe my business partner over here some money, and since you don't seem able to pay, I'm taking enough stock to cover your debt. Makes sense doesn't it?"

"Bumpy, I was just getting ready to put in check in the mail today. See, I have my checkbook right here." She pulled a checkbook out of her coat pocket. "I'll make a check out for three thousand right now."

"You owe five thousand," Perks said.

"Okay, five." Margherite said hurriedly as she began making out the check.

"Pleasure doing business with you, Margherite, as always," Bumpy said after she handed the check over to Perk. "You're a real sweetheart. Give Mayme a call when you get a chance. I'm sure she'd love to hear from you."

Perk, who later opened the famous nightclub Perks Fine Cuisine on the corner of 123rd Street and Manhattan Avenue – became more than just Bumpy's business partner, they became close friends. He may have been one of Bumpy's newer pals, but he was as close and loyal as any of Bumpy's childhood chums. To this day, more then forty years after Bumpy's death, I know I can always count on Perk to come to my aid if I need anything.

Even though Bumpy came home in '63, Nat was still locked up. He'd only been sentenced to ten years on the federal drug charges, but after he did that time they transferred him over to the state to serve out another sentence he'd gotten right around the same time. He didn't get out until after Bumpy died. Obadiah was no longer hustling, and had opened up two diners on 135th Street. He became a respectable business man, though he still came around to see Bumpy from time to time. Wesley Goodwin and John Levy died of heart failure while Bumpy was away. By 1963 Red was back home, and even though he and Bumpy never became friends they developed a very cordial relationship.

Junie, Finley, Georgie Rose, Steve Mitchell, and Ritchie Williams were still very much around, though. Junie and his wife had moved into the Lenox Terrace, a new luxury housing complex on 135th Street and Lenox Avenue, and he urged Bumpy to move in – so Bumpy and I moved into a suite on the penthouse floor.

Life was good again.

Oh, not that it didn't have a few ups and down.

Bumpy had always loved going to Belmont Racetrack – one more thing for my gambling hubby to lay a bet on. We used to go all the time, and he even wrote a sweet poem about how nothing was better in life then spending an afternoon at the racetrack with his beautiful wife. The poem was so good they printed it in Crisis Magazine.

When Bumpy got out in '63, Belmont was closed for some reason – I don't remember why. I think renovations. So he started going to Aqueduct Raceways instead. I didn't always go with Bumpy; sometimes he'd go alone or sometimes he would take a friend. I didn't know that him bringing friends meant lady friends, though. But Bumpy had always been a womanizer, and he wasn't any different after spending all that time in the penitentiary. It was two years after he got out, in 1965, when I found out about one woman in particular whom he was seeing.

It was a Saturday afternoon, and I was having tea with a friend of mine when Bumpy walked in the door with Lena Horne.

"Look who I ran into outside," Bumpy said. "She has to go to the bathroom so I told her to come on up here."

My friend was floored, and Margaret was in awe. Even I was impressed, I was used to having people like Duke Ellington, Paul Robeson, and Cab Calloway in the house, but Lena was in a class by herself. I insisted that she stay and have lunch with us, and she agreed.

As we sat at the table eating and laughing as she regaled us with her Hollywood stories, and life on the road, and we swapped Ethel Waters stories. Margaret, who was about 14 at the time, couldn't help herself; she kept staring at Lena and saying, "You sure are pretty." Both Lena and Bumpy would beam every time she said it, though I couldn't figure out what the heck Bumpy was grinning about.

Then from out the blue, Lena said, "Oh, Bumpy. I must have left my scarf at the racetrack. And that was my favorite scarf. Or maybe I'm lucky and I just left it in your car."

The room suddenly became quiet. I tried to keep my face composed, but my friend's mouth dropped open, and Bumpy looked down at the table. The silence was finally broken when Margaret said, "You sure are pretty. But you're not as pretty as my mama. Right, Daddy?" I think I loved Margaret more that day than ever before.

Bumpy drove Lena home right after that, and when he came home that evening he brought me a beautiful mother-of-pearl necklace and earrings set. I usually made a big fuss over Bumpy when he bought me gifts, but that evening I just nodded and said,

"Thank you, Bumpy." Neither Bumpy nor I mentioned the incident again. I never did wear those pearls. And I never watched another Lena Horne movie.

Chapter Eleven – Farewell to Harlem

Now that we lived at the Lenox Terrace, 22 West, a club on 135th Street became Bumpy's favorite new afternoon hangout spot. He had a booth in the back of the restaurant, and everybody who wanted to talk to him knew to look for him there.

And it seemed like everyone needed to talk to him about something. Politicians looked to him to help get out the black vote, gang leaders came to him to settle disputes between them, and folks in need of a handout came to see if he could spare some money. He always could.

Bumpy especially had a soft spot for the Black Militants who were just making the scene in Harlem. He and Leroi Jones, now known as Amiri Baraka, would talk from time-to-time, and he also knew and supported H. Rap Brown, Stokely Carmichael, and Max Stanford --who first introduced Harlem to the Black Panthers, and later founded the Revolutionary Action Movement (RAM). He used to say he loved their spirit, and said he knew white folks weren't ever going to willingly give up power but maybe they'd do it with a gun pointed at their heads.

In 1965, it was Bumpy who went around to all of the businesses, sporting men, and the East Side Italians to pay for the funeral of a man whom he'd just met but he truly admired. Bumpy was in prison in 1943 when this man, who then called himself "Detroit Red," moved to Harlem. Red was a fast talker who sported flashy zoot suits, flaming red conked hair, and ran

210

numbers for West Indian Archie. By the time Bumpy got out of Dannemora in 1947, Detroit Red had fled Harlem for Boston. But when Bumpy came out of federal prison in 1963 the two finally met. The man's flashy zoot suit had been replaced by a conservative business suit. His red hair went from zonk to a closely-cropped natural. And his fast-talk had turned into long and well-thought out sermons. Detroit Red had become Malcolm X.

Bumpy was impressed with Malcolm, and one of those who supported Malcolm's new organization after he left the Nation of Islam in 1964. When he was assassinated while giving a lecture at the Audubon Ballroom in 1965, Bumpy was devastated. After delivering the funeral money he raised along with his own contribution to Malcolm's widow, Betty Shabazz, he bitterly told Junie, "I offered him protection, and he turned it down. Said he didn't want men with guns around him because it would be like he was trying to provoke something. He shoulda listened to me."

But anyway, everybody in Harlem knew Bumpy, and those who didn't said they did. It was a way of getting what they now call street credibility. And Bumpy was pretty generous with his fame – as long as you don't cross him, pester him, or (sigh!) try talking to a woman he wanted to talk to.

But man oh man could Bumpy hold a grudge. A couple of years after Bumpy got out of prison he heard that New York Charlie – the pimp who testified against Bumpy in '38 – was back in town. Well, his body anyway. He'd suffered a heart attack, and his family wanted him buried in the city of his birth. The funeral was being held at Rodney Dade's Funeral Home, up on Seventh Avenue.

I didn't know anything about it until I was fixing breakfast and smelled something funny – bad kind of funny. I searched the entire apartment looking for the source of the stench, but couldn't locate it. I finally opened the front door, thinking the smell was coming from the hallway. I almost fell out. There, right next to our door, was a bucket of horse manure.

"Bumpy," I yelled out. "Come look at this."

I expected he'd start ranting and raving and trying to find out who would put something like that at our door, but he simply said, "I know. I told one of the kids to get it for me and leave it out here."

"What do you need a bucket of horse manure for?" I questioned him.

"Because I'm going over to New York Charlie's funeral and throw it in his coffin. I couldn't get to him while he was alive, so I'm going to send him to his grave with a little something to remember me by."

While he was in the shower I hurriedly called Junie and he came upstairs and helped me finally talk Bumpy out of it. That Bumpy was something else.

One of the people who really wanted to get to know Bumpy was a country bumpkin from North Carolina. He was a real hick. The rumor was he had to leave the South because he'd gotten drunk and killed a white man's mule. When the white man said he'd wanted the money for that mule or the country bumpkin's hide, the hick told the white man he'd gladly pay him the next day. Instead he managed to get a bus or train up North and wound up in Harlem.

I don't remember who it was that introduced the country bumpkin -- whose actual name was Frank Lucas – to Bumpy, but I do know after they met Frank would hang out wherever he heard Bumpy would be – always asking him if there was anything he could do for him. Bumpy had him take out the trash at Palmetto's, run errands and wash his car, but that was pretty much the extent of it. See, Frank was, well, he seemed rather stupid. There's no harm in someone not being able to go to school, but it was 1965 or '66 at the time – and Bumpy couldn't understand why someone would choose to stay illiterate. I wouldn't say that Bumpy disliked Frank, but he wasn't crazy about him, either. Frank had a way of getting on Bumpy's nerves, always shuffling like he was still in the country, and trying to be so nice he was downright ingratiating. Always, "Yes sir, boss man," or "You sure looking good today, Mr. Johnson," or "Can I get you anything, Mr. Johnson?" He couldn't hold a decent conversation with Bumpy. Bumpy just thought he was funny, and kind of used him as comic relief.

When that article came out in New York Magazine in 2000 -- with Frank saying that he was Bumpy's right hand man, bodyguard and enforcer -- most of the old timers in Harlem laughed. We figured that was one stupid writer who just believed everything Frank told him without even bothering to check. I mean, Frank even said that Wells Restaurant was on Lenox Avenue. The writer couldn't even check that out? And when they did that documentary special on television, Frank pointed out a brownstone on 121st Street and said, "There. That was my boss's house." We never lived on 121st Street, we lived in an apartment building at 2 West 120th Street. But then Frank wouldn't know because he didn't even know Bumpy then; we moved to the Lenox Terrace right after Bumpy got out of Alcatraz. Frank even said he was Bumpy's driver for 15 years. Bumpy was in prison until '63. He died in 1968. What 15 years was Frank talking about? Bumpy had never been out of prison for 15 years straight since coming to New York City.

And the thing was Bumpy didn't have a driver, that man loved to drive, and was always driving other people around in his car. When he went to the racetrack with friends, it was always Bumpy doing the driving. That is, until it wasn't safe anymore.

Bumpy found out when he was in Alcatraz that he had a bad heart, but he didn't start having any real trouble with it until early 1967.

Charlie Coles was a heroin dealer from Detroit, who had only been in Harlem a few months, but he'd already made a name for himself in certain circles. He and Bumpy were okay, but Bumpy wasn't trying to be around any heroin people after that federal frame-up, so he and Charlie pretty much only nodded in passing and then kept going. But in February of 1967 there was a big snow storm, and Charlie was walking along Seventh Avenue on his way home from some club when he saw Bumpy – in the middle of that snow storm – leaning against his Cadillac.

"Hey, Bumpy. You okay?" Charlie yelled out.

Bumpy didn't respond, so Charlie walked closer. He said Bumpy finally looked up at him, walked a couple of steps and then fell into his arms. Charlie hustled him back into his car and drove him to Harlem Hospital. Turned out he'd had a major heart attack. He was in there for a week. Everyone in Harlem tried to visit Bumpy while he was in the hospital, but I was blocked them all. Bumpy needed some peace, and I was trying to make sure he got it. Even Frank Lucas – who I have to admit, really did admire Bumpy -- was trying to get up in the hospital to see him, but I had left explicit orders with the hospital staff not to let anyone in, and not to let Bumpy know people were trying. He was in such a bad way he never even wondered why he didn't have any visitors.

After he got out of the hospital I wouldn't let him drive himself around. Bumpy hated giving up his driving, but he went along with me. After that he would let people do the driving. J. J. was his main driver, and also Big Bobby Jones, but there were two or three times when he even let Frank drive him around.

He was at Aqueduct, with Big Bobby Jones, cheering his horse on when he suddenly keeled over. Bumpy wasn't a small man, but Bobby Jones was a real big man. He scooped Bumpy up in his arms, threw him in the car and high-tailed it over to Queens General Hospital. They wanted to keep him, but Bumpy checked himself out. Bumpy said he was feeling fine and he wasn't thinking about no doctors – that the only thing he needed was a good meal. We couldn't persuade that stubborn man he needed to stay in the hospital, so I just gave up and fixed him a meal. That was in March.

Then in May he had another heart attack while eating lunch at Frank's Restaurant on 125th Street. Bobby Jones was around again, and he was the one who got Bumpy over to Harlem Hospital. Once more, Bumpy refused to stay.

It was a couple of months later that Bumpy got arrested. For drug dealing. And God help me, this time it wasn't a frame-up.

Bumpy had started dabbling in the drug trade about 1965. He still didn't want anything to do with heroin – he thought it was a sucker drug that destroyed too many lives. But cocaine – well, that was different. The thought back then was that cocaine wasn't so bad. People didn't get addicted to the stuff, and while it didn't bring in as much money as heroin, there was still a lot of money to be made. And the Feds, at the time, weren't really concentrating on busting people dealing recreational drugs like cocaine and marijuana. They were after the heroin dealers.

Today, most of the cocaine comes from Columbia. Back then it was produced in Peru. Like heroin, most of the cocaine brought into New York was brought in by the Italians. All of the dealers bought their wholesale drugs from the East Side Italians then peddled their wares on the streets of Harlem, turning a profit of about $10,000 a kilo. Oh, by the way, cocaine was a LOT more expensive back then. Believe it or not a wholesale kilo was going for about $35,000. Don't ask me why, I don't know.

But Bumpy decided if he was going to get into the cocaine game he wasn't going through a middle man. It took him a while, but he made his own cocaine connection with a group of Peruvians. It pissed the Italians off to no end, but Bumpy didn't care.

On the morning of July 8th, 1967, Bumpy was standing by his car in front of the Lenox Terrace waiting on J. J. to drive him over to Palmetto, his exterminating business on Second Avenue. But just as J. J. was walking up, two DEA agents approached Bumpy.

"Bumpy," one of them said, "you gotta come with us. They wanna talk to you downtown."

It must have seemed like déjà vu for Bumpy. But instead of going along quietly like he did in 1951, he pushed J. J. out of the way, jumped into his car and sped off – tires screeching. The Feds took off after him, and called for backup. Bumpy sped down Lenox Avenue, east on 125th Street, and managed to get on the Van Wyck Expressway heading for Queens – speeding the whole way. The police eventually forced him off the road, but Bumpy still had no intention of letting them make an easy arrest. He jumped out the car and started fighting. It took six officers to finally subdue him.

The New York Daily News ran the story in the next day's paper that read:

"Acting on indictments handed up by a federal grand jury, federal narcotic agents yesterday arrested the suspected kingpin of a ring that smuggled many millions of pounds of cocaine in the U.S. Arrested after an 80-mile-an-hour chase along the Van Wyck Expressway for 15 miles was Ellsworth (Bumpy) Johnson, 60, described by authorities as the brains and money behind the largest import of cocaine in the nation."

According to the newspaper story, Bumpy was buying the coke at $20,000 a kilo and smuggling it into the country in the false bottoms of suitcases. Five Peruvians were indicted along with Bumpy. They set bail at $50,000. I bailed him out of jail immediately.

So much for Frank Lucas saying that he inherited Bumpy's heroin empire after his death – Bumpy's only drug business was in cocaine. And so much for Denzel Washington who was playing Frank in that movie, saying in the film that Bumpy was nothing but a flunky for the Italians, and that only he – Frank – was smart enough to cut out the middle man.

Most of the old-time Italians with whom Bumpy didn't mind doing business, were gone. Lucky Luciano and Albert Anastasia, were dead. Joe Adonis had been deported in 1956, and Frank Costello was forced into retirement. The new guys running things had little loyalty to Bumpy, and Bumpy had little loyalty to them. Until the day he died Bumpy believed it was this new generation of Italians, bitter that he was cutting them out of the action, who had tipped off the Feds to his operation.

Bumpy hired a new lawyer, Samuel Segal, to fight the drug case, and things were pretty much quiet for the next year. Bumpy continued in his numbers operations and his legitimate businesses, and he continued to hold court at his favorite restaurant, 22 West. Bumpy still wielded great influence. In fact, when the 1968 riots broke out after Dr. Martin Luther King, Jr. died, it was Bumpy who helped bring about the peace.

John Lindsay was mayor then, and when the rioting broke out that evening he drove to Harlem and tried to calm the rioters down. He hurried up and ducked back in his car, though, when folks started throwing rocks at him. He drove back downtown, and got on the telephone with Harlem politicians, asking them to help out – to accompany him to the streets to help pacify the rioters. One of the politicians told him he'd accompany him, but only if they brought Bumpy along – because no one in Harlem would defy him. Lindsay came back uptown and he and the politician persuaded Bumpy to come out with them. You'd better believe that no one threw rocks this time around. The 1968 riots in Los Angeles and Newark lasted four or five days – Harlem, however, was back to normal by the next morning.

One Friday evening in July Bumpy told me he was just tired, and he was going to call it an early night. I was worried, because this was so unlike Bumpy, but I tried not to let it show. He sat in the living room for a little bit, then said he was going to bed. I said, okay, and reminded him that we were supposed to go to a friend's house for dinner the following night. He kinda grimaced, but said, alright. But then when I climbed into bed about a half hour later he asked me to call and cancel the dinner plans. He wanted to eat something light, and this particular friend was known to make real heavy meals.

"Mayme, how about you just make me some chicken and dumplings tomorrow? I feel like some chicken and dumplings."

I said, "Sure, Bumpy. You want chicken and dumplings, we'll have chicken and dumplings."

218

We'd just got settled in bed when the phone started ringing – Finley asking Bumpy to come on out to a poker game he was holding at the Theresa Hotel because there were some high rollers in town and he was sure they'd come over if they knew the famous Bumpy Johnson was going to be there. So Bumpy got out his bed, got dressed and went out to the game. He got back to the apartment at 3 a.m. and he looked so bad; so tired and worn.

But he got up at 5:30 a.m. like usual on Saturday – it was July 6, 1968 – and was out the door an hour later to take care of his business. He went around to his number spots to make sure everything was in order, then went over at 22 West by noon, as was his usual routine. He came home about seven that evening, and I fixed him a nice hot plate of chicken and dumplings. I was just about to take the telephone off the hook so Finley or nobody could coax him back out because Bumpy was still looking pale and drawn, but just as I reached for the receiver the phone rang. I picked it up and instead of saying, "Hello," I said, "He's not home," and slammed the telephone down. Bumpy looked up from his plate.

"Now what if that was someone important?" he asked me.

"That wasn't anyone important," I said defiantly. "More than likely it was someone wanting some money, someone wanting you to settle some stupid argument they should be able to handle themselves, or someone wanting you to go out and gamble." Bumpy just laughed.

Lawrence Welk was on, and he really loved this rag time pianist, Jo Ann Castle, who was on the show that night. When the show went off, Margaret came in the room and said she wanted to go to some carnival in New Jersey in the morning, so Bumpy said, "Mayme,

219

give her some money tomorrow so she and her friends can have a good time." Then he said he was going to bed. It wasn't but nine o'clock. We lay in the bed for awhile, but Bumpy was restless.

Finally he got up and said, "You know what, Mayme? I'm going to go out for awhile. I can't sleep."

He started dressing, and then opened up our dresser drawer and counted out five hundred dollars. "There's a skin game up on the Avenue. I'm going to go check it out."

"Bumpy, are you sure you feel good enough to go out?"

He said "I'm feeling fine."

"You don't look fine," I said as I followed him to the door.

Bumpy looked at me real funny and said, "I'm feeling fine, Mayme. You worry too much."

I told him again, "You don't look fine." And I started blinking my eyes to work up some tears in them – like I said before, the one way I always knew I could get my way with Bumpy was to put on a good cry – but before I could start the water works Bumpy grabbed me around the waist.

"If I didn't feel fine, could I do this?" He said as he started humming and twirling me around the living room in a slow dance.

"It had to be youuuuuu. It had to be youuuuuuu . . . " he started crooning. "I wandered around, and finally found the somebody whooooooo . . "

I couldn't help myself. I started laughing. "Bumpy, you sound like an old black crow with a sore throat."

Bumpy stopped mid-step, and put on a face like he was hurt. "Aw, see, Mayme, here I am serenading you and you're going to make fun of me."

"Bumpy," I put my hand tenderly on his face, "I'm sorry. You know I was just . . ."

"I may not can sing, Miss Mayme, but I sho' can dance!"

And with that he let go my waist, twirled me around again and started doing the Black Bottom, The Snake, and a bunch of other dances from the twenties and thirties – dances that were in vogue when he was in his heyday.

"Bumpy, you fool!" I shouted through my laughter. "Let me go!"

"Aw, now you see you're jealous, ain't ya?" he shouted. He let me go and then broke out in the Charleston. "Come on, Mayme! Dance with me!"

"I'm not dancing with you. You're plumb crazy." I was rolling with laughter.

Bumpy danced around for another couple of minutes, then grabbed me in a bear hug, and gave me a great big kiss on the lips. I was still laughing, but then he stroked my cheek and in a low voice finished our song,

" . . .for nobody else, gave me a thrill. With all your faults, I love you still. It had to be you, wonderful you. It had to be you."

With that he gave me another soft kiss on the lips, and he was out of the door – before he could see the genuine tears rolling down my cheeks.

We lived on the 17th floor – the penthouse floor – but when the elevator reached the tenth floor the doors opened up and Junie got on. He was a silent owner of the Rhythm Club up on 133rd Street, and he was on his way to stay until closing. He told me later what he and Bumpy talked about that night. Junie told me the story over and over again until the day he died.

"Man, you look like hell," Junie said as he punched the already lit lobby button. "Where the hell you going."

"You know where I'm going," Bumpy replied.

"I know where you should be going. Carry your ass to bed, nigger."

"There's a skin game on Seventh Avenue. I'm feeling lucky."

Out of all of Bumpy's friends, I believe that Junie and Nat loved him best. I always did believe that. Oh, Finley and Obadiah and the rest of them adored Bumpy, and probably would have done anything for him. But it was Junie and Nat that I'm sure that would have jumped in front of Bumpy and taken a bullet for him. They loved him like that. And they knew that Bumpy loved them like that. Out of all of Bumpy's friends, those three – Bumpy, Nat, and Junie – were the closest. That night Junie could look at Bumpy and see that he was in no condition to be going to a skin game.

"You look like shit, nigger. Like I said, carry your ass to bed."

"You sound like Mayme," Bumpy said with a chuckle.

The doors opened to the lobby. But before Junie could get off the elevator, Bumpy suddenly reached over and pressed the "Close Doors" button.

"I need you to do me a favor," Bumpy said after the doors closed. "I want you to take care of Mayme if something happens to me."

"Man, what you talking about? Didn't I take care of Mayme when you went down before? And shit, you know you ain't going down for this shit they got you up on charges for."

"Naw, man. I'm not talking about if I have to do a bid. I'm talking about if something happens for real, Junie."

"Something like what?"

"Something like whatever."

Junie pressed the "Open Doors" button. "I ain't even trying to hear that shit. Ain't nothing gonna happen to you. I gotta get to work. I told them I was gonna be at the club at eleven and it's almost that now."

Bumpy blocked Junie from leaving the elevator. "I want you to promise."

"Fuck you, Bumpy."

"Fuck you, Junie. Make the damn promise."

By this time the elevator buzzer was buzzing through the halls, signaling that someone was holding up its progress. And the doors kept opening and closing, depending if it was Bumpy or Junie pushing the buttons.

"Excuse me. Can I get on?" Junie and Bumpy looked up to see a smiling young man standing in front of the elevator doors.

"Fuck you!" They shouted at the same time. The poor young guy seemed paralyzed in shock, and the doorman rushed up and shoved him out the way.

"Man, I ain't promising you shit!" Junie yelled at Bumpy.

"You supposed to be my man and you can't promise you'll take care of my woman – my wife – if something happens to me!" Bumpy shouted at him. "And you supposed to be my man?"

"You supposed to be my man and you need me to make a promise like that? Motherfucker, we been together since we were kids and you want me to promise something you should already know I would do?" Junie shouted back. "And you supposed to be my man?"

"I am your man!" Bumpy said. "And I . . . and I . . . you know . . . "

"Yeah," Junie said. "I know. And I love you, too."

Junie said they looked at each other for awhile, ignoring that stupid buzzer. "And since Nat ain't here, I'ma tell you like he would if he was here. Youse my nigger . . . "

"If I get no bigger." Bumpy finished his sentence for him. He paused for a moment and added. "You realize I got water on my heart."

"Yeah, I realize," Junie said simply.

"Thanks for realizing," Bumpy said just as simply.

Much to the relief of the doorman, and to the other tenants of Lenox Terrace in the lobby afraid to approach the elevator, the two men finally left the building.

"I'ma give you a ride to the game. Hell, it's only a couple of blocks from the club," Junie said when they were out on the street.

"Great."

Frisco Paddy, a con man from California was at the skin game. Less than three hours later, Bumpy didn't have but thirty-eight dollars left of that five hundred he had pocketed before he left.

"Man, I'm getting up outta here 'cause I'll be damn if I'ma let you take all my paper," Bumpy said about 1:30 a.m.

"Yeah, I'm outta here, too. Wait up," Frisco Paddy said. "I need to talk to you, anyway, Bumpy."

"About what?"

"A friend of mine wants to open a numbers spot. Up on St. Nick."

"St. Nicholas? Shit, that territory belongs to my man, Chink. Chink Cunningham. I can't let you cut in on his action," Bumpy said as they walked out together.

"My friend already got the okay from the East Side," Paddy said, referring to the Italians.

"Fuck the Italians," Bumpy said.

"Yeah, that's why my friend asked me to talk to you."

"You're smarter than I gave you credit," Bumpy said with a smile. "Come on, let's go over to Wells Restaurant. I'm hungry. We'll talk business over a meal."

For all of you readers under age sixty, let me tell you since you probably don't know. Wells Restaurant was the place. *The place.* It was opened by Joseph Wells, no relation to Dickie, in 1938, and quickly became the spot where all the Harlem Sportsmen, what people now call players, met after their game was done. If you were a pimp, a gambler, a con man, a gangster, whatever . . . if you were really in the game, you were at Wells to swap stories, techniques and boasting rights over a meal of fried chicken and waffles. It was just what everyone did back then in those good old days of Harlem. Oh, those good old days.

It was about 2 a.m. when Bumpy got there, and he waved to Finley Hoskins and J. J., both of whom were standing at the bar.

"What you doing here?" he asked Finley.

"Cleaned them out early," Finley said. "There was some high rollers at the game but they left early 'cause your ass wasn't there."

"I can't be everywhere at once," Bumpy said.

"Coulda used you, though," Finley answered as he turned his attention back to his Seven and Seven.

Bumpy sat down with Paddy and ordered coffee, a chicken leg, and hominy grits – Bumpy always like good old southern hominy grits. The food arrived, and Bumpy brought a forkful of them hominy grits up to his lips when suddenly he looked at Paddy, grimaced, then grabbed his chest.

"Bumpy!" Paddy shouted.

Bumpy blinked a couple of times, then slumped from the table onto the floor.

"Bumpy!" Paddy cried again, this time loud enough for everyone in the club to hear.

There was a nurse there, and she rushed over and started massaging his heart. Finley and J. J. rushed over, and Finley grabbed a glass of water from the table and started rubbing ice on Bumpy's forehead.

"Someone call an ambulance," someone shouted.

"Fuck an ambulance. J. J., go get Junie." Finley shouted.

The Rhythm Club was right around the corner, so J. J. was there in less than a minute. Junie said as soon as he saw Frisco Paddy, before Paddy could get a word out of his mouth, he knew what had it happened. He ran out the door and was at Wells' within seconds.

He said when he got there Finley was still kneeling over Bumpy.

"It's too late. He's dead," the nurse said.

Junie ignored her, and scooped Bumpy up in his arms. "I got you, nigger. Don't worry, nigger, I got you."

Junie told me that Bumpy looked at him and smiled, and then gave him a little laugh. And then he closed his eyes.

Junie yelled for someone to call an ambulance and Finley told him that one was on its way. The nurse said again, that it was too late, Bumpy was dead, and Junie – who had probably seen a lot more dead men than that nurse or any doctor – knew that now it was true. But, he told me, he didn't want Bumpy laying around waiting for some morgue guy to take his time getting over there and Bumpy lying there for people to just ogle his body.

"Aw, nah. He ain't dead," Junie told her. "Hurry that ambulance. And someone hurry up and call Mayme."

Cleaver Willis and Bumpy never got along, ever since the day Junie persuaded Bumpy to intercede on Cleaver's behalf with the Italians and then Cleaver went and made peace without telling Bumpy – but it was Cleaver who jumped in his car and sped over to Lenox Terrace.

When Cleaver told me what happened I just threw a big loose dress over my nightgown, slipped into some shoes with no stockings and got outta there. I didn't bother going to Wells'. I rushed right on over to Harlem Hospital. It was only 2:15, less than fifteen minutes since Bumpy heart attack. And understand that Harlem Hospital was only across the street from the Lenox Terrace. But when I got to the hospital Junie was outside, and he was crying. I just looked at him and said, 'Junie, he's gone, isn't he?' and he just said, 'Yeah, Mayme. He's gone.'"

Bumpy's life may have been a violent and turbulent one, but his death was one that any Harlem sporting man would pray for – eating fried chicken at Wells Restaurant in the wee hours of the morning surrounded by childhood friends. It just can't get better than that.

Contrary to all the lies Frank Lucas later told, he was no where around when Bumpy died. And if Junie was alive to hear that Frank was going around saying that Bumpy died in Frank's arms Junie woulda cut his heart out.

Thousands of people attended Bumpy's funeral, which was held at St. Martin's Church on 122nd and Lenox Avenue, and there were dozens of uniformed police officers with shotguns visible on the surrounding rooftops. Don't believe me? They even wrote about it in The New York Times. They must have thought that Bumpy was going to get up from the casket and start raising Hell. But I don't blame them. Part of me thought – hoped – that they were right.

Most of Bumpy's other celebrity friends, however, stayed away – perhaps because he died while under indictment for drugs. Lena Horne, Sidney Poitier, Duke Ellington, Ossie Davis, Count Basie – they all stayed away. Logically, I understand. Emotionally, I'll never forgive them. The Harlem newspapers labeled them all as hypocrites; and that's a lot more tame than what I still call them. Bumpy stood by them, staked them, and defended them to the day he died. And they couldn't even pay their last respects.

Sugar Ray Robinson was there, though. So was Joe Louis. Count Basie, and Eddie Smalls, and so was Juanita Poitier, Sidney's first wife.

Finley, Georgie Rose, Bobby Jones, "Spanish" Raymond Marquez, and Hoss Steele, were a few of the pall bearers; along with William "Pop" Gates, and a few others.

One celebrity who did attend was jazz great Billy Daniels, who was also a good friend of Bumpy's. He sang a stirring rendition of "My Buddy," bringing even hard-nosed street players to tears.

"He chose his course, and he followed it with his eyes open," Reverend John H. Johnson, pastor of St. Martin's Church, said in the eulogy after Daniel's song.

"In a world filled with social contamination and double-talk, maybe there was no other way to be a man."

After the funeral the opulent mahogany coffin was loaded into a long black Cadillac hearse, which then slowly made its way to the Woodlawn Cemetery in the Bronx.

Bumpy had finally left Harlem, and me, forever.

Afterword – by Karen E. Quinones Miller

I can remember when the name Bumpy Johnson first meant anything to me. I was ten years old, and still upset that my family moved from Harlem to the Bronx the year before. I found it hard to make friends and would often convince my mother to let me to take the number 2 train to Harlem to visit my pals from the old neighborhood. On this particular bright sunny day in July 1968, I happily trotted up the subway stairs, grasping the two shiny quarters – my weekly allowance which I planned on using to buy a hamburger and a chocolate milkshake at the Rexall on 125th Street and Lenox.

As soon as I walked up the steps from the station I could see something was going on. Even though it was the middle of the afternoon, the shoe repair store, which doubled as the neighborhood gambling spot, was closed. There were no shiny –faced Nation of Islam brothers hawking copies of *Muhammad Speaks* on the corner. Missing, too, were the winos who usually sprawled on the steps of brownstones, drinking brown-bag wrapped pints of Wild Irish Rose and Swiss Up. Something was up, and it had to be something big. A large group of people was milling through the streets – not a crowd or a mob, like I had seen during the Harlem riots just months before, but something gentler. It seemed like a stream of swaying black faces, all

I pulled on the sweaty arm of one woman to ask her what was going on, but she looked down at me haughtily – readjusted her scruffy brown mink stole around her shoulders with one gloved hand, and gave me a slight push away from her with the other. Undaunted, and still curious, I tapped on the shoulder of a tall freckled teenage boy, dressed in his dark blue suit and a darker blue tie – obviously his Sunday best. "What's everyone standing around for?" I demanded.

On any other occasion I'm sure the teenager would have shoved me away, too, but he was excited, and he seemed to want to share his scandalous knowledge.

"Bumpy's funeral!" he answered me in a loud whisper, as if we really were in church, and not in the

I pulled on the sweaty arm of one woman to ask her what was going on, but she looked down at me haughtily – readjusted her scruffy brown mink stole around her shoulders with one gloved hand, and gave me a slight push away from her with the other. Undaunted, and still curious, I tapped on the shoulder of a tall freckled teenage boy, dressed in his dark blue suit and a darker blue tie – obviously his Sunday best. "What's everyone standing around for?" I demanded.

On any other occasion I'm sure the teenager would have shoved me away, too, but he was excited, and he seemed to want to share his scandalous

"Bumpy's funeral!" he answered me in a loud whisper, as if we really were in church, and not in the

"Bumpy who?" The name was familiar, but I The boy screwed his face up with disgust. Sadly, my question had revealed I was unworthy of his

into a second-floor window better than my Uncle Nicky. But I knew that Bumpy Johnson was a *real* bad man. The kind of man I'd never want to meet.

I wondered if someone had finally shot him. Instead of walking away from the crowd, I was moving further into it as I tried to walk to 115th Street Many of the women were crying, and all of the men had their hats in their hands. I don't know why I looked up, maybe I heard an airplane or the screeching of a bird, but when I did I saw that there were men on the roofs of the buildings across the street from the church. But these men didn't have hats in their hands, they had shotguns. Uniformed police officers with rifles were watching Bumpy

Johnson's funeral. Yeah, I decided, that Bumpy Johnson must have been really bad.

I wiggled through the crowd and over to my friend's house. Soon the tap tap of my double-dutching feet on the sidewalk jarred the thoughts of the funeral out of my head. There was no room in my 10-year-old brain for funerals for people I didn't know, or want to know. By the time I returned home that evening, the whole incident was totally forgotten. It would be another twenty-five years before I thought about that day again.

I was a 36-year-old reporter for The Virginian Pilot, and living in Norfolk, Va., and raising my own young daughter. On this particular night I was doing my weekly ironing, and listening rather than watching, an episode of "Unsolved Mysteries." The episode was about the only successful escape from Alcatraz Penitentiary, which occurred in 1962. The piece suggested that prisoners escaped with the help of a Harlem gangster, who used his connections to have a boat sent out to meet them in the cold waters of the San Francisco Bay. "Harlem gangster," I said out loud to no one. They must be talking about Bumpy Johnson. I was right. I heard the narrator launch into a mini-biography on Bumpy – how he had fought a bloody war with the crazy Jewish mob boss, Dutch Schultz, over control of the numbers racket in Harlem. I knew about the story, of course – everyone in Harlem did. Bumpy may have been unknown to the white world, but in Harlem he was a legend. And I had actually attended his funeral. Well, sort of.

As the show went on, I thought of another Mr. Johnson I had known. A man who once helped me in a way that seemed positively heroic at the time. He'd be the same age as Bumpy Johnson, but the two men couldn't have been more different. I'd lost contact with him a child, and I suddenly regretted it. He was probably dead by now, I thought. I wish I had been able to attend *his* funeral. I met nice Mr. Johnson when I was eight. My mother, my twin sister and my two brothers lived in a three bedroom apartment at 31 West 115th Street, right around the corner from the real estate office where my mother worked as a minimum-wage bookkeeper. One of her sometimes co-workers was a woman I only knew as Madame, who was also the local number runner.

I was a third-grader at P.S. 184 on 116th Street when I stopped in my mother's office to hand her my report card. All 'A"s as usual, but there was something different on this report card. In the comment section it said that I had been selected for the Intellectually Gifted Child program, and that the following year I would be attending P. S. 166 on the Upper West Side of Manhattan. My mother simply gushed when she saw it, and she proudly showed the report card around the office. Madame, whom had never said more than a quick hello to me before, reacted with such delight you would have thought I were her child. She said she wanted to reward me for doing so well in school by letting me hang out with her once in while.

The next morning Madame picked me up in her black Cadillac – she was the only woman I knew in Harlem who had her own Caddy – and drove me around for an hour, making stops all over the neighborhood, without ever saying a word to me until we stopped and got out at Graham Court – a huge apartment complex – at 116th and Seventh Avenue. Oh, God, I was so impressed! Graham Court was huge, and had a gated courtyard with entrances to the four buildings which made up the complex. All of the buildings had locked lobbies with intercoms, like I had seen on television. The doorknobs and railings were shiny brass. The steps were made of veined marble. I had seen the apartment complex all my life, I once lived right around the corner, but I had only dreamed about actually going inside the gates. I was already feeling well-rewarded for my academic achievements.

After we were buzzed into the building on the southeast corner of the courtyard, Madame leaned down, told me to mind my manners, then knocked at the door of a first-floor apartment. A giant of a man with a tiny hat perched on the side of his head, grunted us in. Madame left me sitting in an overstuffed chair in a room full of strangers – mostly men – all waiting around, some playing cards, while she went into a back room. I didn't care for the first half-hour or so, I was busy taking in the apartment. The ceilings were so high I knew even my tall cousin Wesley wouldn't be able to reach it even if he were standing on one of our kitchen chairs. There was a chandelier, the first one I had ever seen, with a hundreds of tiny bulbs. I wished that it was evening instead of in the middle of the afternoon so I could see chandelier shimmer, or perhaps the warm glow of light that I just knew would come from the marble fireplace. I was so impressed with the apartment itself, I took no notice of the furniture. I just knew the person who lived in this grand residence had to be a millionaire. I wondered who it was. Certainly not one of the men who were in the room with me. They were big rough-looking men, not the kind of men who could be the master of this magnificent home.

I wondered if instead it was one of the people in other room who were speaking with Madam. I couldn't make out what was being said among the raised voices, save for Madam, attempting to "explain" something. Fifteen minutes later, a distressed looking Madame walked back into the living room along with three men. One of them was Mr. Johnson.

He was dark-skinned, with hair so short he looked bald, and dressed in an elegant dark blue suit. When he entered the living room, everyone stood up. He paid them little attention, he looked angry, and was walking, fast, toward the front door when he suddenly noticed tiny me in the large over-stuffed chair.

"Well, hello there," he said his face breaking out into a crinkly nosed smile.

"Ke-Ke, sweetheart, say hello to Mr. Johnson," Madame said, suddenly all sugar. "Mr. Johnson, I'll have you know that my little Ke-Ke is the smartest little girl in her third-grade class."

Even as young as I was, I suddenly realized that Madame had brought me to the apartment because she knew Mr. Johnson, would be angry with her about something, and she also knew that Mr. Johnson couldn't stay angry around children. I found out later that Mr. Johnson loved children. Especially smart children who liked to read Langston Hughes. He actually knew Langston Hughes, he told me at that first meeting. I was impressed. The one question I had, I blurted out immediately.

"Is he nice?"

"Real nice," Mr. Johnson answered with a laugh. "Go get this smart young lady some ice cream." As if by magic, there was suddenly two bowls of vanilla ice cream on a large mahogany dining room table.

"What's wrong," Mr. Johnson asked as I slowly picked up my spoon.

"Um, I like chocolate."

"Don't be rude, Ke-Ke!" Madame said sharply.

"Go out and buy Miss Ke-Ke some chocolate ice cream," Mr. Johnson said, his smiling eyes never leaving my face. "I like young ladies who aren't afraid to say what they want."

Our relationship was cemented over ice cream, vanilla for him, chocolate for me.

It was the first of many visits that summer. Each visit would begin with a sometimes heated discussion between Madame and Mr. Johnson, and end with Mr. Johnson and me sitting at the table eating ice cream while he told me stories about Langston Hughes, and other literary figures of the Harlem Renaissance, most of whom

I didn't know. But his friendships weren't just limited to writers. Mr. Johnson said that he was good friends with the famous boxer Joe Louis, and that he had been best pals with Bill "Bojangles" Robinson, the man who tap danced the steps with Shirley Temple. I was in total awe. I always hated when our visits ended, and would pout when Madame said it was time to go. But Mr. Johnson would smile and pat me on the head saying, "You know you're going to be seeing me again, Miss Ke-Ke."

It was towards the end of the summer when Mr. Johnson sat me down and gave me a good talking to when he found out that I had been selected to go to the white school downtown because I was an "Intellectually Gifted Child," but didn't want to go.

"Miss Ke-Ke," he said puzzled over my hesitation. "This is the opportunity of a lifetime."

"I don't want to go," I insisted as I gulped down the bowl of chocolate ice cream he always kept on hand for my visits. "I don't want to go to school with a bunch of white kids."

"Why not?" he insisted.

"Because."

"Because what?"

"Just because," I said, giving him my pat 8-year-old answer to all unanswerable questions.

But Mr. Johnson had a way with children, and it didn't take long before I was confiding in him that I thought the children at P. S. 166 on 84th Street and Columbus would laugh at me because I wore hand-me-down clothes that my mother didn't have time to mend. Even the children at P.S. 184 laughed at me, and their clothes weren't much better.

"Miss Ke-Ke, you don't go to school to show off clothes, you go to learn," Mr. Johnson admonished me with a quiet smile. "But I know just how you feel. The kids in my school used to laugh at my clothes, too."

236

Harlem Godfather:
The Rap on my Husband, Ellsworth "Bumpy" Johnson

I looked at him incredulously. First of all, I never considered that Mr. Johnson could ever have been a child. I wasn't good at guessing ages, but I figured he must have been as old my grandfather would have been if he were still alive. Secondly, I couldn't even imagine anyone teasing Mr. Johnson about his clothes. He was always dressed so nicely, always in a suit and tie, and even at eight, I could see that his suits and ties were very, very expensive. And of course, he must have been a millionaire – after all he lived at Graham Court.

"Kids laughed at you because of your clothes?" I asked suspiciously.

"Yes, they did, Miss Ke-Ke."

"And what did you do?"

"I beat them up."

There were a bunch of men in the apartment – Mr. Johnson always had at least two or three really big burly men with him – and they hollered with laughter at his answer until he gave them a silencing glare.

"Now, I don't want you go around beating people up, Miss Ke-Ke," he said returning his attention to me, "because you're a smart young lady, and smart young ladies should fight with their brains. But you have to go to school to learn how to do that. And you have a chance to go to a really good school. Don't let the thought of people laughing at your clothes keep you from learning."

I was pretty much convinced. Clothes or no clothes, I was going to that white school and get as smart as Mr. Johnson, and maybe I would get to meet people like Langston Hughes and Bojangles, and live in a grand apartment, too.

Madame stopped coming around my mother's house to pick me up, and the rumor on the street was that she had been sent to prison for something or the other, so my visits to Mr. Johnson's house stopped. But two weeks before school started there was a knock on our apartment door. My mother answered it, and a man gave her a white

envelope that was marked "From Mr. Johnson." Inside
were five crisp twenty-dollar bills, enough in 1967, to buy
really nice school clothes for me and my twin sister and
two brothers.

******

My thoughts were jolted back to the present when
my cat suddenly leaped onto the ironing board, almost
knocking down the iron. I took it as omen that I needed a
break from housework. I walked into the living room and
plopped down on the couch in front to the television just
as a black-and-white mug shot of the infamous Bumpy
Johnson appeared on the screen. I couldn't believe my
eyes, it was my Mr. Johnson. I couldn't believe my eyes,
or my ears as the announcer called him the "most
notorious gangster in Harlem."

The television show went off, but not before citing
a book on which the episode had been based. I hurriedly
scribbled down the title, *Riddle of The Rock: The Only
Successful Escape from Alcatraz*, by Don DeNevi. I
hurried to the bookstore that very afternoon, and bought
the book, and devoured it within hours. There was only
one chapter on Bumpy Johnson, but there were two
photographs of him. Yes, there was no doubt that it was
my Mr. Johnson. I puzzled how the nice old man who had
been so good to me could be the fierce criminal of Harlem
lore. The more I puzzled, the more determined I was to
find the answer.

And thus my odyssey began.

Shortly afterward I was hired by The Philadelphia
Inquirer, and so was able to travel to Harlem three or four
times a week. I went to the Schomburg to learn everything
I could about Bumpy, but sadly, there wasn't much. On a
hunch, I looked up Ellsworth Johnson in the telephone
book and found that there was still a number listed in his
name. I called the number, hoping to find one of his
children had kept the number. When a woman picked I

blurted out, "I'm sorry to bother you, but I'm looking for the residence of Bumpy Johnson."

There was a pause, and the voice said, "This is his widow. May I help you?"

Mayme Johnson and I spoke for hours, and she invited me to come meet her, although she wouldn't be available for a few days. I happily agreed.

The following morning I went to meet with John Henrik Clarke to interview him for a story I was doing for The Philadelphia Inquirer. After the interview was over I casually asked him if he knew Bumpy Johnson, and he told me that not only did he know Bumpy, he greatly admired him.

Clarke was one of the most well-known African-American historians living – part of the so-called Black Intelligencia – and I astounded that a man of his stature would admit to admiring a gangster. When I told him this Clarke laughed and said, "There's always going to be gangsters, and there's always going to be those who exploit others, but Bumpy never took anything from anyone who couldn't afford it. And he always gave to people who were in need. They used to call him the Black Robin Hood."

The problem with Harlem, he went on to say, was that Bumpy was no longer around. "These punks out here now think they're gangsters, but they're nothing but hoodlums. Bumpy would put them in line in no time flat."

Now I was really intrigued. In the coming months I managed to find Junie Byrd, Finley Hoskins, and a few other of Bumpy's cronies, and to my delight they were more than willing to talk about their old pal. Finally, I was getting a fuller picture of Bumpy Johnson.

Because we could never get our schedules in sync, I wasn't able to meet Mrs. Johnson face-to-face for almost a year. When we did meet I found her to be a charming and warm woman – and we quickly became friends. We discussed me one day doing a book about her husband, but she was always too busy to give me an in-depth series of interview, and soon my own career as a novelist began taking off, so we put the biography on hold.

In 2004, Mrs. Johnson moved to Philadelphia, to be closer to her daughter, Ruthie. Now I was able to visit with her every day. Once again we discussed doing the book, and I even wrote a book proposal and submitted it to book publishers. But while they said they found the story interesting, they didn't think enough people would care enough about Bumpy Johnson to actually buy the book.

Mayme Johnson and I disagreed. And if you're reading this, obviously you do, too.

Thank you.

.

LADIES . . . DON'T LET YOUR HUSBAND OR BOYFRIEND READ THIS BOOK! SOME SECRETS NEED TO BE KEPT TO OURSELVES!

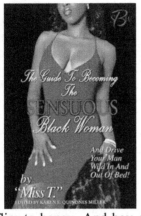

Ever wonder why some women seem to get all the men? Even the ones who are no where near as good looking as you? Wondering what it is they've got that you don't? They're tuned into their SENSUALITY, meaning they're in tune with their senses, their body, and they know how to receive and give pleasure. Men can intuitively spot these women, and they're drawn to them like flies to honey. And boy do these women know how to dish out the honey! These are The Sensuous Black Women, and you can join their number by reading **"The Guide to Becoming The Sensuous Black Woman (And Drive Your Man Wild In And Out Of Bed!)"**

Tips include:

- How to Attract a Man From Across the Room

- Been Bad While He's Been Away? How to "TIGHTEN" it up so

   he'll never know!

- Want Your Man To Taste You Down There? Make It Tasty!

- Put His Condom On For Him -- Using Your Mouth!

The Guide to Becoming The Sensuous Black Woman (And Drive Your Man Wild In And Out Of Bed!) **is available in bookstores nationwide, including Borders and Barnes & Noble or at your favorite online store!**

Mayme Johnson
and Karen E. Quinones Miller

Raw: An Erotic Street Tale

Money make me cum – money, money make me cum .

Chastity Jones is the real thing. She's beautiful, she's classy, and she's got money to spend. Other people's money. As long as there are men around, 19-year-old Chastity will be rolling in their dough.

It wasn't always like that – her father was sent to prison when she was 16, and after being placed in a foster home, she was brutally raped. She runs away, and starts stripping at a men's club, and there she catches the eye of Legend, a mysterious and handsome 6-4 hunk with straight black hair that hangs over his shoulders. His brownstone parties are famous – attended by celebrities, ballers, and hustlers alike. But the real parties are in his basement; sex parties that include girl-on-girl action, and even occasionally bestiality. His parties are so successful he easily clears $25,000 to $40,000 a weekend.

For Chastity it's love at first sight, but try as she might Legend only treats her like a little sister –and under his tutelage Chastity is soon hanging with the big dawgs. They buy her cars, pay the rent on her condo, buy her expensive jewelry and take her on shopping sprees. But the man she wants most shows her no romantic interest; and that's Legend.

And then she meets Hunter – he's a drug kingpin with millions of dollars, and also Legend's cousin – and he falls for Chastity in a big way. Suddenly Chastity is caught up in a whirlwind of money, sex, drugs and danger – and the only way out lies in death.

http://facebook.com/rawgirl

Harlem Godfather:
  The Rap on my Husband, Ellsworth "Bumpy" Johnson

Made in the USA
Coppell, TX
19 July 2020